1,000,000 Books

are available to read at

Forgotten Books

www.ForgottenBooks.com

Read online
Download PDF
Purchase in print

ISBN 978-1-331-69210-2
PIBN 10222174

This book is a reproduction of an important historical work. Forgotten Books uses state-of-the-art technology to digitally reconstruct the work, preserving the original format whilst repairing imperfections present in the aged copy. In rare cases, an imperfection in the original, such as a blemish or missing page, may be replicated in our edition. We do, however, repair the vast majority of imperfections successfully; any imperfections that remain are intentionally left to preserve the state of such historical works.

Forgotten Books is a registered trademark of FB &c Ltd.
Copyright © 2018 FB &c Ltd.
FB &c Ltd, Dalton House, 60 Windsor Avenue, London, SW19 2RR.
Company number 08720141. Registered in England and Wales.

For support please visit www.forgottenbooks.com

1 MONTH OF FREE READING

at

www.ForgottenBooks.com

By purchasing this book you are eligible for one month membership to ForgottenBooks.com, giving you unlimited access to our entire collection of over 1,000,000 titles via our web site and mobile apps.

To claim your free month visit:
www.forgottenbooks.com/free222174

* Offer is valid for 45 days from date of purchase. Terms and conditions apply.

English
Français
Deutsche
Italiano
Español
Português

www.forgottenbooks.com

Mythology Photography **Fiction**
Fishing Christianity **Art** Cooking
Essays **Buddhism** Freemasonry
Medicine **Biology** Music **Ancient Egypt** Evolution Carpentry Physics
Dance Geology **Mathematics** Fitness
Shakespeare **Folklore** Yoga Marketing
Confidence Immortality Biographies
Poetry **Psychology** Witchcraft
Electronics Chemistry History **Law**
Accounting **Philosophy** Anthropology
Alchemy Drama Quantum Mechanics
Atheism Sexual Health **Ancient History**
Entrepreneurship Languages Sport
Paleontology Needlework Islam
Metaphysics Investment Archaeology
Parenting Statistics Criminology
Motivational

237
G658
144790

BOOK 237.G658 c.1
GORDON # QUIET TALKS ABOUT LIFE
AFTER DEATH

3 9153 00066632 3

QUIET TALKS
ABOUT
LIFE AFTER DEATH

S. D. GORDON'S
QUIET TALKS

Quiet Talks on Power
Quiet Talks on Prayer
Quiet Talks on Service

Quiet Talks About Jesus
Quiet Talks on Personal Problems
Quiet Talks with World Winners

Quiet Talks About the Tempter
Quiet Talks on Home Ideals
Quiet Talks About Our Lord's Return

Quiet Talks on Following the Christ
Quiet Talks About the Crowned Christ
  of the Revelation
Quiet Talks on John's Gospel

Quiet Talks on the Deeper Meaning of
  the War
Quiet Talks About Life After Death

Quiet Talks About Simple Essentials
Quiet Talks About the Healing Christ

QUIET TALKS
ABOUT
LIFE AFTER DEATH

BY
S. D. GORDON
*Author of "Quiet Talks on Power,"
"Quiet Talks on Prayer"*

NEW YORK   CHICAGO   TORONTO
FLEMING H. REVELL COMPANY
LONDON AND EDINBURGH

opyrig t, , y
FLEMING H. REVELL COMPANY

Printed in the United States of America

New York: 158 Fifth Avenue
Chicago: 17 North Wabash Ave.
London: 21 Paternoster Square
Edinburgh: 75 Princes Street

CONTENTS

	Preface	7
I.	Death, the Ceaseless Tragedy of Life	11
II.	Those in Touch of Heart with God Who Have Died—What Can We Know Certainly About Them?	17
III.	The Others Who Have Died—What Can We Know Certainly About Them?	93
IV.	Can We Have Communication with the Dead?	124
V.	What Is Death?	154
VI.	Is There Another Chance for Salvation after Death? . .	167

PREFACE

The world is still in the back-wash of the war. The big boat's gone by, but the suction behind at her stern is terrific. And we're all having a time of it trying to sail across its rough wake.

Whether it's statescraft, or what passes for statescraft, or economics, or just plain bread and bed and coal, we've all got our hands full, clean to the fingertips, trying to keep afloat, and not to be sucked under, either financially or morally. For these seem the two deepest suctions in the wake of the boat.

Religion's in the tug, too; or rather, religious moorings. The real thing itself is safe enough. But our connections sometimes seem pretty shifty and uncertain.

No statistics can count up the dead. Violence and disease, gaunt want and strain, have formed their old alliance, not to mention what's going on all the time. And their slain outdo our figuring.

We're close up to old Egyptian times,—"Not a house where there was not one dead," almost; ofttimes more than that. And the pull upon one's emotional nature is tremendous, while brave hearts go bravely on doing faithfully the day's common tasks.

But to countless numbers the questions, the old questions, old as time almost, keep pushing in night and day: Where is he? Is there life beyond? If so, where and what? Can we get in touch across this stubborn barrier—death? Should we, even if we could?

Imaginative speculation regarding the dead, spun, pretty much, like the spider's web, out of the bowels of one's own wishes and longings, spreads like wildfire. The absence of facts, or rather the persistent ignoring of facts, seems to fertilize its rapid over-night mushroom growth. And these mushrooms are of the deadly sort.

The unhallowed "strange fire" has swept over the church and the land, on both sides of the water, like the unchecked dreaded wildfire of the prairie. And, mark you keenly, it's not merely a matter of belief like an article in one's printed creed, recited either more or less by rote. It gets to be a matter of morals, or the lack of morals. For belief and character are inseparable twins. One's real creed is spelled out in the syllables of his daily contacts. And right well the crowd knows it.

The connection between attempted, so-called, communication with the dead *and* demon activity is as old as sin, and as subtle and certain. The present movement is uncanny in the rapidity of its growth. It is plainly devilish in its origin and growth and influence.

One clear gleam of good sunlight will cut straight through a skyful of graceful, graytinted clouds. One good whiff of sharp, bracing air will send the rose-hued clouds helter-skelter. They're pretty, those vaporous clouds, brewed up out of sunless dank lowlands and swamps, but how they do vanish into thin air, as though ashamed, before clear sunlight and vigorous wind.

Preface

One fact, simple incontestable fact, puts these unwholesome spinnings of imaginative speculation clear out of the running. Happily there are facts, clear, well-established, indisputable facts, fully sufficient to satisfy the keenest brain, and cushion and comfort the torn heart. They give the distinct key-note for joyous singing in the midst of cloud and shade.

An astronomical expert had gone to Egypt to superintend creation of a telescope. He noticed that the military post fired a gun at noon every day. He asked the officer in charge how he got the accurate time for the noon gun. He got it from his watch. And how did he correct his watch? By the watchmaker in Cairo. A few days later he inquired of the Cairo watchmaker how he got his correct time. *"By the noon gun!"* was the reply. Is this the way some do in the serious things, the moral things? Each keeping tab with the other, and no stabilized recognized standard form to go by?

As one who has felt, into the marrow of the bone, the stinging slash of death brushing rudely by; and who knows, too, and knows certainly, *Some One else* coming and staying closer by, with his insistent message of settled certainties, I have tried to gather up here, in simple shape, the clear proven facts. There is quite enough, a big enough, to give sure footing and glad singing as we go about the daily task and through the constant tug. We are blest in having a standard to measure by, a Book that stands giant-like above the crowd of theories and opinions.

It will be noted that I have *paraphrased* a good

many passages of Scripture to get clearer the meaning of the original language underneath our English. A paraphrase is a translation of the *thought* rather than a literal translation of word and sentence.

In their thoughtful effort to avoid any possibility of seeming to lean this way or that, doctrinally, the translators of our English Bible have been compelled to make what, ofttimes, practically amounts to a literal translation. In the New Testament, for instance, the translations, remarkable in their accuracy and spirit, are frequently Grecized English rather than idiomatic English.

And so the paraphrases have been worked out here to give more simply and fully the *thought* underneath the English. The utmost studious painstaking care has been taken to make these paraphrases strictly accurate to the Hebrew and Greek text being quoted.

Quotations are from the American Revision except where otherwise noted.

I

DEATH, THE CEASELESS TRAGEDY OF LIFE

Commonplace, But Always Sacred

It was almost four on a September morning. A young man in the vigor of his strength was walking slowly out a deserted street of one of our Atlantic seaboard cities.

The gray was well streaked up the east. The new day was pushing away the dying night's blackness. But he scarce noticed it, if at all. He was too much taken up with another conflict of light and night, in his spirit.

His step was slow, his head bent. A deep mood gripped him hard. He was in the heavy daze of something new, that is, it was new to him. His house was not far from a famous park. A small quiet graceful stream ran through it.

He climbed the green-clad hill where the city's water was stored. It overlooked the river beyond, with the wavy mass of the quieting green of the tree-tops nearer. He drew a little limp-covered book from his pocket. And he sat down, by turns, looking out over the green and the water, reading in the book, looking up into the blue.

A few hours before a life had slipped out of

his clinging grasp. He had clung tenaciously. But softly, gradually, insistently, her spirit had slipped away and was gone. He was dazed with surprise and grief. It had never occurred to him that she would die. He had held on with love's unyielding hold till there was nothing left to hold on to. She was gone. Only the breathless bit of a precious form remained.

They two had been as closely knit together in spirit as two ever were, or could be. But now she was gone, gone quite beyond recall. That was clear, quite clear. He was outwardly very quiet, attending to the things that needed doing.

But within he gasped. He could not seem to get his breath. All life was changed. The world was a different place. She was gone. The daze of it was thick upon him; not stupefying, no, making him keenly sensitive and alert in spirit, more than ever.

Now he sat still. The question asking itself of him—where is she? The precious bit of tenemental clay was there, tenderly cared for. But where was *she?* Not there; somewhere; where?

The little book seemed to open itself at John, the dear old John story of Jesus. And it seemed to stay open as readily at that unforgetable Bethany page, the Eleventh Chapter.

A new soft light shined in upon, and then out of, the old words. And a quiet peace came stealing in, a new peace, sweeter, realer, in the overwhelming daze that well-nigh swamped him.

But a great lone feeling gripped at his heart, mingling with the peace even while yielding to it.

Death, the Ceaseless Tragedy 13

He can't remember how long he sat. Then he climbed slowly down the hill, back along the street they had so often walked together hand-in-hand.

Back he went to the old house and the old round, but to a changed life. It would never be the same again. It couldn't be. He had entered into the sorest experience of his life. He has never forgotten it. Its memory clings still as fresh as though but yesterday.

> "The lights are all out
>   In the mansion of clay;
> The curtains are drawn,
>   For the dweller's away;
> She silently slipped
>   O'er the threshold by night,
> To make her abode
>   In the city of light."

And yet how commonplace! Yes, commonplace in its commonness, *its frequency,* monotonously commonplace. No, no, quite wrong, never commonplace, sacred, hallowed, a thing quite by itself in its loneliness and grief, though it happen every hour of the day, to some son and daughter of man.

For death is the commonest thing in life. Its shadow never leaves. The postman puts the black-bordered reminder into your hand. The caller's card has the same touch. The garb you passed just now on the street, the half-masted flag, the tolling of the church bell, the low requiem breathing out the church windows, the slow-moving procession—these are daily things.

Commercialism halts the telegraph system of a

nation a scant five minutes to tell out honor to some one gone, and then picks up its mad rush again. The trolleys and trams at a brief stand still, the white monument draped in black, and public buildings covered with the clothes of grief, these tell the same ceaseless story.

If you open the old Book, it's barely open before you hear Eve's sobs over her boy lying so still. Almost at once you are in that striking Fifth of Genesis with its requiem of sorrow chanting monotonously, "and he died."

The despairing cries of a race going down under the great wash of inundating waters, and the wail of broken hearts in Egyptian homes over the first born gone, catch your sensitive ear.

If you hurry on through the pages to get away, it is but to hear the dear old Singer of Israel sobbing his heart quite out over his handsome self-willed boy.

And the newer leaves open with the cries of the broken-hearted mothers of little Bethlehem among the hills. The symphony of sorrow seems never to get to its end.

Death Always a Tragedy

And death is always a tragedy to somebody. Life is tragic. Death seems but the dark double-knotting on the end of the tragic thread of life. Never a day passes without death breaking some heart. Never a corner safe from the dripping rain of death's tears sometime.

Homes are broken up. The hearthstone is left to its white ashes. The dear loved family circle is scattered beyond reunion here. Habits of a life-time are snapped in their toughest threads. Plans and ambitions lie scattered to the mocking winds. And memory trails its minor chords along every street and hallway of the bruised heart and rudely disturbed life.

The world's worst war has added a terrific emphasis to all this. It was bad enough before. It is running riot now, seemingly an unchecked, unrestrained, ghoulish riot, despite statesmen and law-makers, armistices and treaties, and all the rest.

But there is something yet more tragic than these things. There is the terrific uncertainty in most minds and hearts growing out of these things. Uncertainty, where the heart's involved, where love's on tenter-hooks, that comes to be the worst pain that can come.

The questions come trooping in, insistently, incorrigibly, by day and by night, demanding asking space, and giving no breathing room inbetween. Is he still alive? Is there a spirit world? Is there really something beyond this life? Where has he gone? How are things with him now?

All over the world, Orient and Occident, below the equator and above it, in savage krall and cultured home, among so-called heathen peoples and in the shining of the flood light of truth, the cry breaks out of human hearts, *where has he gone?* Sorrow makes all the race akin. Differences, hatreds, prejudices, are submerged in the hour of a common sorrow.

Yet there's clear light. There's an answer to

these questions. There is certainty in the place of uncertainty. There's positive dependable information at hand. It's enough to give the golden tint to every black cloud. There's another bit of music that comes to overcome minor chords in the symphony of sorrow, even while these still give their sweetened underchording to the new joyous rhythm.

And of that certainty we want to talk a bit now. We want to find the keynote of the mingled symphony where joy sweetens sorrow, and sets your hearts a-singing and a-tingling, through the bit of waiting for the reunion day.

> Fierce was the wild billow,
> Dark was the night,
> Oars labour'd heavily,
> Foam glimmer'd white,
> Trembled the mariners,
> Peril was nigh;
> Then saith the God of God,
> "Peace! It is I!"
>
> Ridge of the mountain wave,
> Lower thy crest,
> Wail of Euroclydon,
> Be thou at rest.
> Sorrow can never be,
> Darkness must fly,
> When saith the Light of Light,
> "Peace! It is I!"
>
> Jesu, deliverer,
> Come Thou to me,
> Soothe Thou my voyaging
> Over life's sea;
> Thou when the storm of Death,
> Roars sweeping by,
> Whisper, O Truth of Truth,
> "Peace! It is I!"
>   Hymn of St. Antolius.

II

THOSE IN TOUCH OF HEART WITH GOD WHO HAVE DIED—WHAT CAN WE CERTAINLY KNOW ABOUT THEM?

The Oldest Question

Where is *he?* There's a narrow pine box, and a slender strip of green sod. But *he* is not *there.* Or, *is* he? *He,* where is *he?*

It's the oldest question, that is the oldest tense human question. It has been wrung out in every generation by grief, staring dry-eyed or sobbing, over the sod strip, out into the gray beyond.

Our earliest mother knelt broken-hearted by the body of her boy. It was a triple grief with her. Her boy was dead, grief enough that. But it was through passionate violence, and, worse yet, violence by his own brother. War had an early start.

Grief had its first birthplace in a mother's broken heart. No, not its first. Its first birthplace was in the heart of God, when His prodigal world went away from the old fire-side. But then that was a mother-heart—a father-mother heart, and a broken heart too.

Yet, it was the first *human* heart. And again you must say, not even that. For God's heart is a human heart, as well as more. We get our human heart from His human heart, we made in his likeness.

That question, and that grief, have never quit since that day just outside the Eden gate. The grief sobs out its ceaseless requiem regardless of clock or clime. And the question intrudes its sharp cutting point into the most sacred hour and corner.

The Greeks were masters of the world. Their sense of beauty has never been surpassed. Their chiselled marble, chaste architecture, and noble teachings, set the world's standard. But their answer to this old question couldn't still the tumult in their own broken hearts.

Quite gone, he had, they said. It's the end. There's nothing beyond. So their brains, though their hearts never accepted the answer. There was a sharp break between the two, never bridged by any philosophy.

Others of them disagreed. But the best thing they could do was picturing a cheerless, aimless, colorless existence that was itself repellant. That was the best answer that the best Greek wisdom and culture could bring.

The Romans were masters of force, sheer brutal force, organized with rarest skill. Their force mastered the Greeks but it couldn't force any mastery here. The question forced them to admit themselves mastered, out-done, in the presence of its breaking grief. They trod the same path hewed out by Greek philosophy. They had no light to relieve the gray gloom.

The earlier dwellers on the Nile saw no better light. They could pierce the sky with their rare pyramidal engineering. But their longing tear-bedimmed eyes could pierce ahead past the line of the grave not the tiniest scratch, nor the faintest gleam.

The Euphrates sages stopped dumb at the same place, hoping, wishing, wondering but skeptical. The Phoenicians could shape an alphabet to be carried through one national culture after another up to our own English. But they couldn't shape a teaching about the future that could ease the heart tug at the gateway of the grave.

And the later teachers up to this hour, following the same path of reasoned research, have nothing to add to those earlier thinkers. The best they can bring is a vague uncertainty. Wearisome comforters are they all, like Job's friends.

The candle's snuffed out. He has gone, for good and all. That's the end. *Or,* you can dimly see him wandering aimlessly about in a gray gloom that only adds a touch of bitterness to the heart's grief.

It's a cheerless answer. The cold light of reason is well called cold. This is the best and the most that its lantern can do, or, at any rate, has done, in the night of man's sorrow. It's a repellant look out into the dark night.

But stop. That's not all. There is another answer. And it's an answer that answers. There's no beggarly begging of the question here. And it stands in sharpest contrast to these others. They are vague. It is positive and clear. There's an element of thoughtful measured certainty, that begins to ease the heart at once.

Indeed certainty is a marked characteristic of this answer. There is a sheer certainty that is startling *and* refreshing. Already the air clears. The clouds scurry. Sunlight begins to edge the clouds with its cheery golden glint.

A Small Group of Facts

There is a small group of facts that underlie this teaching of certainty about the life after death. A fact is something that is really so. It stands in direct contrast with theory or speculation, with mere logic or argument. A fact is a real state of things. It is something to be reckoned with in practical life. It is something you can put your finger on and say "this is so".

The sun is a fact. You look up and see it. There it is. The theorist explains that you really don't see the sun. For it is some ninety-two or -three million miles away. And the human eye cannot see that far. It's the reflection you see. And he is quite right in his theorizing.

But the crowd, busy with its daily practical work, is impatient of mere theory. It says, "there's the sun in plain sight, you can see it. You feel its heat. You work by its light." And that settles the thing. The crowd pushes ahead with its work. And the crowd is right. The sun is a potent fact in common life.

Now, to the plain man on the street, too busy for fine-spun theory, there is a small group of facts that stand out to common view as plainly as the sun in the sky. And one's daily life can be shaped by them as really as by the sun.

First of all, *Christian civilization is a fact.* It stands out in sharpest contrast with the civilization of the Caesars, which overspread the world in the time of Christ. Treatment of the weak is the acid test of any civilization.

Then, there was slavery both white and black. Now, there is not only freedom from slavery, but the highest civil rights for the humblest and state education for all, from the poorest up.

Then, woman was a chattel, a piece of property merely. Now, she is loved, shielded, cultured, queen of the home, and more. Then, children were commonly despised and neglected, when not actually thrown to a horrible death. Now, they are prized and cared for as our most precious possessions.

Then, degrading superstition controlled in the care of the sick, and the mentally deficient, when they were not wholly ignored. Now, science and a gracious humanitarianism combine their best, even in caring for those who can offer no compensation.

Then, the most sordid unadulterated selfishness held complete sway. Now, actually billions of money are given voluntarily for the relief of the needy. Then, there were no commonly accepted standards of morality. The question of sex morality was quite commonly regulated by the fact of property rights, or ownership, as is quite common to-day where Christian civilization does not control.

Now, in all the lands known as Christian, there is a standard touching the great moral questions of truth and honesty and right sexual relations.

That standard is continually violated. But it is recognized, and has an incalculable influence in common life.

Take these few items simply as threads in the whole fabric of similar weave. It is not possible to state the case fully in brief words. For Christian civilization is an atmosphere filling the lungs of the western world. We are too much a part of it to sense it fairly. Only a Roman, dropping down into it, could appreciate the tremendous contrast, as he tried to catch his startled breath.

The contrast is stupendous. These things, and the like, are recognized as the distinctive traits of Christian civilization. The contrast in this regard between western nations and those where Christian influence has not yet permeated, is both painful, *and* is a living exposition of Christian civilization.

And all this is in spite of the fact that our Christian civilization has just suffered its most savage, most unchristian, most uncivilized, blow; and that too, from within itself. It is in spite, too, of the fact that the present day feverish restlessness among so-called Christian nations brings sharply to view conditions and practices that are decidedly non-Christian.

Indeed the question has been freely raised how far our boasted Christian civilization is mere veneer, of varying thickness, for something radically different underneath; a pretense covering up something that needs hiding. This tree seems to have grown great until birds find their nests in its protecting branches, foul scavenger birds, preying on human kind.

But Christian civilization is not an original thing. It has not an independent life. It has no roots of its own. It is an outgrowth of something else. And that something else is greater than the outgrowth. The root is more than the shoot growing out of it, immensely more in this case.

If some yet more savage war swept over the world, and stuck to its job longer, and cleaned the whole thing of Christian civilization out of existence, the root out of which it grew would still remain. It would remain as full of life and fertility as before. It would put forth new shoots. And its growth would again largely cover the earth.

Christianity a Fact

This leads to the second fact, *Christianity is a fact*. For Christian civilization is an outgrowth of Christianity. Christianity is the root. Christion civilization is the shoot out of the root. It has no separate life of its own. And more yet, it seems pretty plain that Christian civilization isn't the chief outgrowth.

These radical differences between two civilizations must really be classed as *incidentals*. Revolutionary they are, blessedly revolutionary, yet mere by-products. Christian civilization is a by-product; nothing more. It is a by-product of Christianity. It is not the main thing itself.

For, by common consent, no nation to-day is Christian in the profession and daily lives and practices of even a majority of its people. And the governmental policies, while taking on the outer coloring of Christian civilization, are underneath, confessedly the reverse of Christian, in the selfish, grasping spirit that dominates. Christianity has not had the opportunity of producing its chief result in the generic life of Christian nations.

So, if these distinctive traits of our characteristic civilization are mere incidentals or by-products of something else, that something else is seen to be not only a fact, but a fact of immensely deeper significance.

Christianity is an *ideal, a group of moral principles,* and it is a vital *power,* that makes that ideal and those principles real in human life. It can change radically a human life from bad to good. And it *does* it. It presents a high ideal, makes a man long intensely after it, and then makes it an actual experience in his life, overcoming the most stubborn opposition.

No stronger thing could be said of any power. It changes the human will. It changes it at the core. And it does it wholly from within. There is no other power known to man that has done that, or that can do it.

The drunkard becomes sober, and a hater of the evil he once loved so passionately. The impure becomes pure, the thief honest, the covetous generous, the wavering and drifting purposeful, the weak strong. And the changed man becomes a new factor influencing his surroundings.

Every continent, and civilization, and distinct race, has living evidence of such change. Yellow men and brown, black men and white, have alike revealed this unmatched solitary power at work.

The extremes meet here. The city slum, that ugly ragged sloughed-off edge of our best civilization, and the savage tribe untouched as yet by *any* civilization, acknowledge alike this transforming power.

This is what I mean by saying that Christian civilization is merely an incidental of Christianity. This thing of changing radically human character from bad to good—this is the chief thing. *Any* thing else is incidental to this. The civilization is mere surface veneer. This goes down to the very vitals. Indeed this is the starting point of a true abiding civilization.

And so, Christianity is seen to be a fact, in plain open evidence in the life of the race. It is an indisputable fact even to those who hate it.

Christ a Fact

But there's another step in the ladder. Put your foot up on the next rung. Christianity leads you straight to something else. And again it is something else greater than itself. It's a sharp scale ascending. The something else proves to be some One else. For Christianity doesn't stand by itself. It is not a thing nor a system in itself. It is merely a shoot out of a root.

As Christian civilization roots in Christianity, so Christianity roots in Christ. It comes out of Him. The two are intertwined beyond separation. And it is less than He. The shoot is less than the root. Cannon Liddon said a few generations ago, "Christianity is Christ." That is, the real thing of Christianity can be understood only as one gets to Christ. He is the standard of it. And so we have the third fact. *Christ is a fact.*

I am ignoring a whole lot of evidence here. There are large evidential reserves wholly untouched. I am talking for the man in the street, on the move, to be caught by plain talk if at all. Simply from this level, where all are compelled to confess what their eyes see, Christian civilization certifies the fact of Christianity. And the fact of Christianity certifies the fact of Christ.

And Christ stands here not simply for those thirty-three years of His personality. Christ stands for the potent influences that radiated, and that radiate, from that personality, and from those years with their tremendous happenings.

The name Christ stands for ideals, the highest known. It stands for ideals lived amid the stress of our common life; actually lived. It stands for love and sacrifice beyond what any other did show, or could show. It stands for power in overcoming the terrific moral inertia of life, the prejudice and superstition, the hatred of men, and of evil at its deadliest, and immensely more in completely overcoming the power of death itself, and living again a new triumphant life on earth past the grave line.

Yes, Christ stands for more yet, the power that can make that ideal a living reality in human life to-day. For what has been said of Christianity must be said of Christ. He is the power of Christianity. Christ is Christianity, the real thing. He is more than it. For all of its power comes out of Him. Christ is a fact, a tremendous, unmistakable, unalterable fact.

The evidence is plain and open to the man in the street. A glance at the date line in the morning paper, and at the post-mark of the last letter that came, tells of the fact of Christ. A touch with some one you know who lives the real thing, or, who has been blessedly changed in life, makes that fact take hold of your very heart.

But there's another egg in this nest. A little mothering will bring it to life. The fact of Christ is linked up with another fact, the Christ-Book. The Bible is a fact, tied and knotted up with the fact of Christ. The two are inextricably interwoven. For Christ is the very heart-blood of this Book. Take Him out of it—you cannot, simply *cannot!* You would have itself taken out of it.

It is striking that you must go to this Book to get the essential facts about Christ Himself. It is the one original source of information about Him. The very book that tells at first hand about the divine Christ must itself be divine. It is a lonely book, solitary, quite by itself in its standards, its ideals, and its power. It would take a Christ to make a Christ. And it would take a Christ to make this Christ Book.

Inspired Revelation a Fact

The Bible is a fact. I do not mean merely that it is a fact that there is such a book. But this Book itself is a living fact or factor in Christian civilization, in Christianity, in Christian propaganda among non-Christian peoples, in the personal history of Christ Himself, and in the human lives it has touched and moulded.

Wherever it is known, it is accepted as the one standard of moral teaching, unapproached by any other. By common consent its contributions to jurisprudence, to political economy, to moral philosophy, business ethics, sanitation and hygiene, are the underlying foundation of all books on these subjects. It is characterized by a fine reserve, a conservative caution of utterance, and a rare modesty about itself. Its high moral character is freely accepted wherever it is known.

In its ideals of life, unmatched and unapproached, its originality, its unfailing freshness and adaptation after centuries, its subtle real touch of something more than human through the human medium, and in its one outstanding person—Christ, it stands in solitary grandeur among all books of whatever time or clime. The Bible is a fact in the life of the race.

And, now, there's another hatch in this brood. A bit of heart warmth will quickly pip the shell. Notice a striking thing. This conservative Book makes a certain claim for itself. It actually claims to be a distinctive revelation from God Himself.

It claims to be so in-breathed by the Holy Spirit as to be a dependable revelation of God's will and purposes, and of how He sees that things will work out. And it is so interwoven with these other plain facts that the acceptance of them, at once, involves the acceptance both of it, and of its claim.

In Touch with God

And so, very quietly, a *fifth* fact adds itself to the group. *It is a fact that there is a revelation from God.* I know of course that this is disputed. It is disputed vigorously with bitterness and persistence. Indeed the peculiar spirit of bitterness and stubborn tenacity in the propaganda against this fact is distinctively unscholarly in spirit, and more, it is suggestive of the real source behind all this sort of thing. There's a bitterness of hate, a serpentine quality of subtlety and venom, immensely suggestive.

But the bit for the common man on the street, who wants things simple and plain and straight, is this. The fact that there is a revelation from God is as clearly a fact as these other facts named. It's as clear as the fact of the sun overhead.

A man may rest in this, as a mere matter just now of flawless logical reason, that the acceptance of these facts is in full accord with the most rugged intellectual integrity. The most vigorous insistent mentality can rest content in following this simple line of reasoning. Merely as a *matter of evidence*, regardless of the moral consequences involved, this group of facts may safely be left to the verdict of the highest judiciaries of these two English-speaking peoples.

Muddy Scholarship, and the Real

I have put the thing in this simple direct positive way because of the muddy scholarship that has such wide sway to-day. That is, it passes for scholarship, and it is certainly muddy. It is marked by the absence of clear vigorous thinking, and of clean-cut utterances.

There has grown up a system of instruction which uses the fine old name of scholarship. It sits in high places, in universities and divinity schools. And its text books and influence are in the lower schools. Its dominant method is to raise questions and leave them hanging in the air, the biggest thing in view. With elaborately spun speculation, which has a fine scholastic tinge and tang, it incubates doubt. And the incubated brood far outnumbers those of a natural mother, as in many a commercialized poultry yard.

In choice scholarly language, with impressive repetition of names prominent in the modern scholarly world, it breathes out a gray be-dimmed foggy atmosphere of doubt. Such authenticated facts as would conteract their theories are ignored, or minimized, or skilfully slurred over.

It has become a common thing for young people, trained in Christian homes, and in simple old-fashioned church circles, and in the old-fashioned beliefs in the essential facts of Christian truth, to be inoculated with these germs. The disease becomes chronic, and a break of moral fibre is a result not slow in arriving.

We must all be grateful for true scholarship. Our debt to it can never be paid. It is striking to note that the best scholarship of the ages is headed in point of time and of preeminence, by one who may be thoughtfully called the greatest of all scholars. And his scholarly research work brought him to the acceptance of a direct distinctive revelation from God.

He was learned in all the vast learning of the Egyptian schools, which were the world's universities of that day. And he had more than learning. He had that rare scholarly instinct for independent research regardless of where it leads, which constitutes the real scholarly genius.

He went to the original sources as has none other. Following the Egyptian University work, and the long post-graduate course in the University of the Desert, were two exceptional post-graduate courses, of six weeks each, most intensive research work, *on Horeb*. That was indeed a going to the original sources.

Real scholarship's results are close at hand in every library of standard works, for him who wants the facts. And nothing is better settled than the utter dependability of this old Book, and the essential accuracy of its transmission to us. We have the Book's message with remarkable dependability and accuracy, as it came from God to and through its writers, under the holy spell of God's Spirit.

That there is a revelation from God is a fact. That fine word revelation is used here in its old-fashioned full meaning. There's no thinning out or watering of its meaning, after modern usage. It is a revelation of something that could have been gotten in no other way.

It is a something that never *has* been gotten in any other way. It does not belittle reason. It uses and honors reason. It is meant to fit into reason's processes. It meets reason at the line of reason's highest achievement, and leads it into higher fields.

Reason with its marvellous God-like powers, slowly works its way up to certain conclusions, and then stops. It must stop. It can go no further. This revelation tells what reason cannot find out, because of its natural limitations. Reverent God-touched reason accepts reverently God's revelation, and finds it in complete accord with, and supplementary to, all that itself has done, and in revealing what it could never find out. *This is the fact of revelation.*

Further, it is noteworthy that this revelation is in full accord with the moral character of the Book which contains it. It is in perfect accord with the character of God and of Christ. It is such a revelation as one would rationally look for from such a source. In this it stands in sharpest contrast with other literature dealing with such matter.

The Bible Practical
―――――――――――

Now it is very striking to notice that this revelation, the old Book of God, deals with the very questions that have puzzled men in every generation. It answers fully this old question, *"where is he?"* It brings the comfort of certain knowledge to the bruised torn heart.

It deals with the questions which the war has brought up all afresh,—the other, spirit world, of which this one we know is only a part, life beyond the grave, communication with the dead, and this whole group of intense questions. In short, it starts in where reason is obliged to confess itself unable to go further.

It answers them with a certainty that is nothing less than startling. And so it is in sharpest contrast with the long line of merely human philosophizings. It comes with a great sense of relief, of refreshment, and, more, of real comfort and strength.

And as one actually lives the fine habitual surrender to the mastery of the Lord Jesus, as he grows keener and more disciplined in his mental processes, as he becomes more sensitive in spirit to the presence and will of the Holy Spirit within himself, the more does his inner spirit answer to the living Spirit within this Book, touching all points of this revelation. And the surer becomes his inner spirit of the reality of God, and of the spirit world.

We turn now to this solitary Book of God. And we bring this oldest tense human question *where is he?* At once you are conscious that here the whole outlook is changed. It is as though you had stepped in out of the night into a house flooded with light.

The whole view-point is diametrically opposite. Outside you seem groping in darkness, or twilight, or early dawnlight. God is left practically out of the reckoning, out there. Here God is let in. He is let in at His own valuation. Once admit God, and the whole equation is changed.

The personal equation, that is, the God equation, completely alters the problem, and its solution. What is impossible without God, becomes the natural thing once God is admitted. It seems so natural now that you know instinctively in your spirit that *God belongs in.*

We find at once that this is a Book of thoughtful distinctions. It doesn't slur moral matters over. It makes a clear distinction between men, based on their attitude of heart toward God and good.

And so the answer to the question is in two parts. The second part is the painful, hurting part of the answer. That will come in our next talk. Just now we want to talk about the first part of the answer. What do we certainly know about those *in touch of heart with God,* who have died.

Our Question Answered

And, I think it may make things stand out clearer, if, first of all, I tell a simple connected running story of what happens to these at death, without using references. Then we will gather the great teaching passages out of the Book, with chapter and verse, and then gather up certain outstanding events or incidents of the Book, that illustrate and emphasize the teachings. The story grows wholly out of these teachings and events.

At last then we come to answer the question, *where is he?* And one may well get into some quiet corner, where he can think quietly, and try to *take in,* the wondrous story that answers the question.

The moment of death has come. The physician, standing so impressively still, with his trained finger on the pulse, says in a hushed voice, "he is gone." *Where?* The beginning of death is the beginning of life. The close here is the opening there. The end is really the beginning. The shutting door to us is an opening door to *him.*

At once, quicker than you can bat your eye, or catch your breath, he is consciously in the immediate presence of our glorified Lord Jesus Christ. He doesn't go alone. A convoy of bright-faced angel-beings meet him, and take his spirit straight up into the presence of Christ in the homeland.

I said *at once.* I said it thoughtfully. I was using the language he and his angel convoy would use. He doesn't travel what we think of as a long distance through space. He is instantly at his new destination.

Time and space and distance are things that belong to our thinking down here. It takes such and such a length of time, we say, to go such and such a distance. That is necessary earth talk. Up there, in the spirit world, they go as swiftly as thought through what we call a long distance. We can't take it in possibly, but it is clearly so.

And so the moment he has gone from us here, he has arrived there, in the new home. He sees Jesus. He meets the loved ones gone before. There's the wondrous reunion *at once.* He hears strains of music such as his human ears have never heard.

All pain of body, all distress of mind, all strain of spirit are all gone. He is at home in a new world, where life and light, harmony and glad joy, are the very atmosphere to an extent we simply cannot take in down here. His cup of enjoyment and happiness is full.

That is a general statement of what has come to him the instant he slipped the tether of life here. Now there are certain detailed particulars of intense interest, of which we have equal assurance.

He is the same person that we knew down here. His *identity* is unchanged and undisturbed. The same essential characteristics, the same individualities, that mark him to his loved ones, remain. All the traits that go to make up his distinct personality remain the same. All distinctive moral traits of a weak or not good sort are gone. But through all the growth and development which now goes forward there will persist the same identity of person as we knew here.

Closely allied to this is the matter of *mutual recognition*. One of the commonest of questions is about knowing each other up there. There is nothing clearer and surer than this thing of instant full mutual recognition. We shall be more over there, not less, our powers keener and more developed.

But, you are thinking that years have gone, by earth's reckoning of time, since they left us. *We* have changed, perhaps very decidedly. And they have changed too, have they not? you say. The possibility of meeting the one tenderly intimately loved without *instant recognition* comes with a sharp sense of pain.

A mother thinks of her babe, perhaps, who died in infancy. The little one had already wound its tendrils so tight in and out about the mother heart. Not unlikely she thinks still of a little babe. Yet she would be grieved and startled beyond words, after years of separation, to find her child a little thing quite undeveloped.

Well, a little thought reveals the comforting truth. Over there in His presence is fullness of life. Our spirit perception will be far keener there than here. Our loved ones will have *grown*, and in the growth all that is best has developed, and developed with the distinctive individual traits.

That mother, as she crosses the threshold of the real life, if not before, will instinctively recognize that her babe has grown, much more, and better, and differently, than if here. She will be looking to meet her child, now matured, cultured, poised, grown with the fine growth of all spirit and mental and individual traits. There will be the intense desire to have it so.

And it is so that she will meet her child. There will be instant recognition that this thoughtful matured manly man, this womanly woman, grown into the fine spirit image of Christ, is her child of the long years ago. And with the recognition will be great joy because of the growth. The recognition will be instant and mutual and joyous.

Now, further, as he comes into Christ's presence there will be *no discussion of his sin*. For he, this man we are talking about, was in touch of heart with the Father. And the sin question has all been settled for him.

Christ's death and resurrection settled it. The blood of Christ covers his sin. And he is accepted by the Father even as His Only Begotten is accepted. He begins to appreciate now just what a tremendous thing Jesus did for him in dying.

But there will be *certain changes* in him of a moral sort. As he comes into the presence of Christ, certain things in his character will be removed or changed. It will be done just as putting a lump of gold ore into the fire instantly makes a separation of whatever there is in the ore that is not gold. The other part is burned up, or thrown off.

Christ is pictured as a man of Fire. Fire purifies. Fire consumes what can't stand the heat of its flame. Christ's mere presence will act on one's character as he comes into that presence, just as the actual fire acts upon the lump of gold ore.

Whatever in a man's character, of the sort characterized by Paul as "wood, hay and stubble," that is, whatever won't stand the fire of the pure presence of Jesus, will be removed as by the burning of fire. That is, whatever there is of selfishness, self-seeking, pettiness, uncontrolled passion, self-will, bitterness, narrowness, the artificial and the like, will go.

It is to be feared that in some cases the fire will burn up more than it leaves. For fire is relentlessly truthful and honest. No doubt many a man's life, (that is, the opportunity of his stay on the earth), will be practically lost because it has been controlled by un-Christlike motives.

But his soul, or after-life, the man himself, will be saved. For that is a matter of Christ's blood. Indeed some will be saved because of what the fire does. For not even Christ's blood can save the growth of selfishness encrusting this man, who at heart really does trust Christ. The blood saves the man himself, the fire burns up these bad growths. There will be some pretty severe shrinkage in the presence of the purifying Man of Fire.

The Changed Outlook

Then, too, the *whole outlook* changes up there. It will be like climbing a high mountain, above the cloud line, after living down here in the valley among fogs and mists. We shall know fully then, even as also we are fully known now. The point of view completely changes. Our sense of values will instantly change, both shrinking and growing.

Everything is seen up there at its real valuation, that is, God's valuation. Some things that we cling to with desperation will be seen as quite valueless. And things that we dimly recognize as good yet let slip, or held with a loose hold, will now be seen as purest gold, of highest value.

We shall see clearly even as now God sees clearly. Things of the earth life, controlling motives, policies of men and groups and governments, individual suffering, the common acute problems—in all this, there will be a radical reshift in values.

This sense of the change of values will be revolutionary. It will come to many with unspeakable tensest surprise, and even shock, this utter shift of values. Yet it will at once be recognized that now things are seen at their true value.

Then the change of outlook will affect our

understanding of *our loved ones still living down on the earth.* We shall be fully conscious of things on the earth. But we shall see all things from God's point of view. We shall understand much, at least, of God's general plans for the future. We will sense how things will turn out.

And if one thinks, naturally, how can we know without being disturbed of our loved ones having difficulties and pain and the like, let it at once be recalled that we shall see all these things from God's standpoint. There will be an utter change of proportion in estimating these things. It will be the true proportion. What holds God steady now in his tender love for us, and yet His intimate knowledge of things here, that same thing will hold us steady.

Then, we want to remember that our loved ones up there in the homeland, *are growing.* We know it by simple inference. For growth is a law of life. And up there they have the real article of life. Whatever has God's touch upon it grows. And up there is God's own fireside. All things are His way. And so there is growth of the finest truest sort, up there.

The dear wee babies, the vast majority of those who have gone through the upper doorway, have been growing. Like the child Jesus, they have grown in wisdom or understanding, and in stature, and in favor with God and men. That covers their mental and spirit and social powers. Under the touch of God's creative power, ever at work, and under the tutelage of their angel-teachers, they have steadily grown in matured, poised, gentle strength.

And so each one has gone on growing in all the fine traits and powers and understandings and self-control, that make perfect human character. For heaven is a school as well as a home. Only both words take on a fineness of meaning there, unknown here. All the fine training of perfect school-life and all the true sweets and restraints of fine home-life are the blessed commonplace up there.

We have all suffered a good bit, including God, by the common teachings about heaven. It has been preached and taught and hymned away out of touch with true human feelings and thought. I can recall distinctly a few lines of a hymn I knew and sang in my early growing days. The lines that still stick in my memory said,

> "Where congregations ne'er break up,
> And sabbaths have no end."

The melody was a fine one. I loved it. I find myself singing it now sometimes. The melody has kept the words living in my memory.

But when I thought into it as a boy it didn't awaken any special enthusiasm over going to heaven. The sabbaths I knew had some unnatural restraints about them, though I still think that those restraints that irked were very decidedly better than the looseness that everything runs to now.

I had a boy vision of one ceaseless church service, on plain hard wooden benches with straight stiff backs, singing psalms and hymns and listening to long proper sermons, and the like. That's a very simple thing, perhaps childish. But is it not of a piece of the common idea most folks have about the other life.

I presume the writer of those lines, like many in the same list, was thinking only of the perfect harmony up there, the sweet fellowship of men with God. But the way he expressed it doesn't seem to fit into human ideas of things we common folk have.

No, it is God's real home up there. Things are as He plans. There's what would be called a natural round of life up there. God is a rhythmic purposeful God. And so there is purpose and motive and definite aim in each life. There's a working toward a goal, and the zest of seeing things grow under one's touch. For that belongs to true life.

Each one yonder has his task and round of occupation, and a rare joy in doing it. It's a busy purposeful active life, up there, but without any strain or worry, crowding or drudgery, or competition of the hurting sort.

Service According to Ability

Then there's another thing to be said with some emphasis, and yet said gently. It is said with emphasis because it seems never spoken of. It is said gently because it touches one of the sore spots in our common Christian life. And the touch may make somebody a bit sensitive, and possibly may hurt a bit. Yet the surgeon's knife that cuts is to prepare the way for healing and health.

The word is this, their occupation **up** there, and the privilege of personal service for the King, will be *according to ability.* But ability has a new meaning, not used down here much. It refers to the *spirit traits* one has grown down here.

Those who, in the stress of life have been true to the Lord Jesus here have grown certain traits of character. There has been a cultivation of the inner spirit life which in turn has given color and shape to the outer life. In following fully they have had difficult experiences on the earth. There have been oppositions and persecutions, sometimes of the subtler sort that cut deep.

There has grown a sensitiveness of spirit to the Master's presence and voice and way of doing things. So there has been grown unconsciously, largely, the traits needed in the Master's upper service. The vision has been cleared, the ear trained for his voice, the spirit keen to understand, the judgment disciplined, the mood made like His own, responsive to Him, and to those in similar touch with Him.

May I say, very gently, that it seems pathetic how many there are whose one thought seems to be to be sure they'll be saved? The thought of being serviceable to the Master *after* being saved seems to slip quite out. There's a natural concern over personal salvation, of course, till it's settled right.

But so many seem to think that having fixed up the matter of salvation, very much—I am putting it bluntly—as you take out any insurance policy, they are free to go on their selfish worldly way, like the outer crowd. The motives of the world seem largely their motives. It's hard to find the difference.

Now, the point to stress is this: our life there, and our privilege of personal service for the King, will naturally be moulded on our Christian lives here. It will be reckoned a great honor, the outstanding honor, to do errands, carry out commissions, and be entrusted with bits of service.

And mark you keenly, *all may serve* up there, who will. There will be no favoritism shown. But of course, only those will be sent on some honored errand who *can* do it, who have grown the traits of character it calls for.

It seems quite clear that when our Lord Jesus does come again (whenever that may be), in the second phase of His coming back to the earth to heal its hurt, He will be accompanied, not by all who are saved through His blood, but by those who being saved, are also *"chosen* and *faithful."* That is, in their life on the earth, they have answered the *call* to personal salvation. They have been *chosen* for some bit of service, *and* they have been *faithful* to their Lord in doing what He asked.

Now, this will naturally be the simple law of service up in the home-land, and in the coming kingdom time. Those are entrusted with doing the king's errands, who have grown the traits needed. And those traits are grown in our earth life by the simple full following of our blessed Lord Jesus.

Yet, let it be carefully noted that every cup of happiness will be full up there. There will be different sorts of cups, varying sizes, and full recognition of the differences, yet each will be as full as it will hold. We shall be absorbed with our glorious King. There will be sweetest fellowship, and fullest accord. Yet some will be honored in service as others cannot be. And the right of this will be readily acknowledged by all.

But, it does look sometimes, as though there'd be a lot of people saved as though by the skin of their teeth, in Job's words. They're in, but barely in; saved, but barely saved. Christ not only had to die to get them saved, but has to burn off a lot of stuff accumulated down here that can't get over the door sill up there.

This seems to be the simple picture etched out before our eyes in this old Book of God. There's much local coloring to add to it. But this answers the age-old question about our loved ones, in touch of heart with God, who have died.

Now Turn to the Book

And now we want to turn to the Book directly for *the detailed study* out of which this simple picture is drawn.

It will be noted that these old Hebrew Scriptures, the Old Testament, are flooded with *the Kingdom conception.* The continual thought absorbing these writers is not death and heaven and the life beyond. They are absorbed with a new condition of things coming on the earth.

There's a King coming, and through Him a

kingdom. And the kingdom they are thinking of will be on the earth. The triumph of right on the earth is their overmastering thought. This prevailing outlook of things is based distinctly on promises to Abraham, and David, and the other fathers of their people.

It is really the same as with the writers of the Newer Testament, where the dominant thought is of some One coming back to the earth, to righten all wrongs and Edenize the earth again. This kingdom conception and outlook in the older pages color all the sky continually.

This makes the references to the future life stand out in sharper relief. Indeed the broad view seems to make it clear that these old writers didn't discuss the future life much. *They took it for granted.* This is the setting of the particular passages we want to look at.

It will be noticed that there are other things taken for granted. *God is taken for granted.* He is above any such thing as death. We are His creatures, breath of his own breath. We have the same quality of life as He. We have been badly hurt by sin. As a result there is death for the body. But the principle of life within us is of the same essential sort as God's. We are kin in the quality of life, through His gracious creative touch. All this is the common background here.

The other world is taken for granted. There *is* another world, another bigger part of this world we are in. It's another sort of world, that part we don't see. God's home or fireside *is* there. There's no death there, with God, for

He talks to successive generations. Men come and go on the earth, but this One is continuous. In very homely simile, it is like the harvests coming and going, but the farmer continues season after season. This, be it keenly marked, is the common point of view of this old Book.

And God is directly concerned about things here. It seems quite natural to them to write down, "and God said," as they do countless times. Jacob is awed by God speaking to him at Jabbok, but it never occurs to him to question it. Abraham's heart is stilled when God appears in a dream or vision, but he accepts it as a thing to shape his plans by.

And *death is taken for granted,* as a dreaded passage through to something beyond. It is something unnatural, a break. It is a thing to be dreaded in itself, like passing through a dark gloomy valley on your way to the mountain top. This is revealed incidentally in the language used.

For instance death is commonly spoken of as *sleep*. Sleep is a temporary thing. It is followed by waking. There is no direct analogy to death in nature. Winter is not death, but sleep. The spring is the waking time with all the powers renewed and refreshed. The grain of wheat is said to "die". But the process it goes through is a natural stage in the getting of the harvest. The death stage that man knows is an *un*natural thing, a sharp rupture in nature's order.[1]

Now, here in the Book, death is as sleep.

[1] Genesis ii. 17 1. c.

The kings are commonly spoken of as sleeping with their fathers. Jacob says "when I sleep with my fathers." David cries out joyously "I shall be satisfied *when I awake,* with thy likeness."[1] This is as common in the Old, as in the clearer resurrection light of the New Testament.

And it should be noted that this usage of sleep for death is distinctive to this old Bible. That is, it seems to have *originated* there. Its use elsewhere is a copy of this old Biblical usage.

Some Incidental Teachings

There's a group of *incidental teachings,* that touch the subject indirectly. Incidental evidence is always strong evidence, like Ehud's left-handed thrust. It reveals an atmosphere, an attitude, an outlook, which at once tells the dominating faith. Look at a few of these incidental teachings.

In the creation story, it is said that God breathed into man's nostrils the breath of life. The lower animal creation had come earlier. Here is something distinctly additional. God's own breath was breathed into man. Man is of the essence of God, *creatively.* We are as God in the possession of life, the fact of life, and the sort of life. This is creative. It is quite distinct from redemptive action. The creative, sustaining, preserving, power of God continues in spite of sin. It's a bit of the love of God.

In the outstanding Fifty-third of Isaiah there

[1] Psalm xvii. 15.

stands an incidental word of significance, "when thou hast made his soul a sin-offering (put to death) he shall see his seed, he shall prolong his days." The same is repeated a few lines farther down. Because he poured out his soul unto death, therefore will I divide him a portion with the great, and so on. Here is not only life after death, but a victorious triumphant life after a peculiarly humiliating death,[1] indicating the continuation of life after death had control.

In that remarkable last chapter of Daniel, there is clear teaching of a coming resurrection, with its direct implication of a continuation of the life of the spirit while the body mingles with the dust. "Many of them that sleep in the dust of the earth shall awake; these (that awake) to everlasting life; the others (that do not awake at this time) shall be to shame and everlasting abhorrence."[2]

And an incidental bit spoken to Daniel personally, closes that chapter, "Thou shalt rest, and shalt stand in thy lot at the end of the days." Or paraphrased, "thou shalt die, but when these events occur thou shalt be living and be in thine allotted place.[3]

It will be noticed that the large group of teachings about the resurrection become invaluable indirect evidence. Clearly if there is a resurrection, it is based on a continuation of the human spirit whose body is lying in the grave.

[1] Isaiah liii. 10-12.
[2] Daniel xii. 2 translation of Tregelles, the famous Hebraist.
[3] Daniel xii. 13.

The resurrection involves a continuation of individual identity, for each spirit re-enters its own body. It takes for granted a spirit world, and that all in touch of heart with God who have died, are in His immediate presence, and that it is His resistless power in action overcoming the power of death.

All reference to the expected Second Coming of Christ belongs in this group of incidental teachings. Whatever view we may hold to-day regarding that subject is quite immaterial, just now, in this connection. Clearly in these pages there was a living faith in His return. His appearance was a thing expected in that generation.

These references at once express belief in the fact of an unseen spirit world, where Christ was then living in the same body they had seen and touched after his resurrection. Those who had died, who were in touch with Him, were in that spirit world. They would return with Him in great victory and gladness.

It will be noted that Jesus' constant standpoint is this: He had come down from His Father's immediate presence, on an errand to the earth. When the errand was done He would go back home again. That made the spirit world a very real thing to Him. The characteristic phrase "eternal life," original with Jesus and the Gospels, carries with it the same significance.

In Peter's address, on the occasion of the healing of the lame man at the beautiful gate of the temple, he says of Jesus, "whom the heavens must receive until the times of the restoration of all things whereof God spoke by the mouth of His Holy prophets."[1] There was clear teaching that the Jesus whom they had killed was living then, up out of view, and living such a life of power that He would be returning to take control of things down here.

In his long teaching letter to the disciples in Rome, Paul makes two incidental allusions full of suggestive meaning. The sufferings then being endured by some of Christ's followers were intense and real, but they are said to be insignificant when compared *"with the glory* which shall be *revealed to us-ward."*

And in the same paragraph there is a most touching reference to the whole lower creation. It is said to be full of inarticulate groanings, the suffering of intense birth-pains, in anticipation of a coming new birth which would include the whole creation, with man himself.[2] Not only is there life beyond death, but a victorious life in which all wrongs are righted, and the earth's hurt healed. This is a gathering of some of the indirect incidental teachings.

Outstanding Passages—Job

We come now to the *great outstanding teaching passages*. It will be noted that these are not isolated texts, picked out. Rather they are some of the peaks of the mountain ranges. Peaks and mountain range are parts of the same thing.

Turn first of all to the Book of Job. There is good reason for accepting Job as the earliest

[1] Acts iii. 21.
[2] Romans viii. 18, 22, 23.

of all the books, in its writing. If written by Moses, as is the early reliable tradition, and altogether likely, it would reveal not only the conviction of the patriarch Job himself, but of the scholarly Moses who chooses this incident for his remarkable essay on the problem of suffering. It reflects the common belief of the early twilight of the race. Or, should we more properly say, before the early creative floodlight had dimmed.

There are two outstanding passages here, both from the lips of Job himself. The "if-a-man-die-shall-he-live-again" passage,[1] and the other "I know that my Redeemer liveth."[2] These two famous bits that have been quoted so much, seem at first flush to be on opposite sides of the question in point. The first seems plainly to express doubt, or, at least, a question. The second rings with assurance.

The two really must be taken together. It seems quite clear that they both were spoken within an hour's time in the running conversation of these four men. As they are talking the cutting replies of his critics have turned the sick man's mood so that the second bit, the "Redeemer" passage seems to be merely a shift of emphasis, a making intenser the statement already made in the first passage.

If one read the question "if a man die shall he live again?", in its connection as it stood in their conversation, it seems plainly to be, not a question of uncertainty, but rather an affirma-

[1] Job xiv. 14.
[2] Job xix. 25-27.

tion, a confession of his faith that he was confident he would live again.

Notice, the *preceding* paragraph[1] is taking the lower view of things as seen on the earth. The tree dies and is gone. The man dies and is seen no more on the earth, just like the tree. But in *this* paragraph containing the question,[2] the point of view is clearly shifted. There Job is speaking to God. The point of view is wholly changed. It's the upper, the higher view.

Listen: "Oh that thou wouldst *hide* me in the world of departed spirits.

That thou would keep me secret (hidden in safety[3]) until thy wrath (in straightening out wrong) be past.

That thou wouldst appoint me a set time, and (then) remember me!

If a man die, shall he live? (I am so sure of it that)

All the days of my present time of apprenticeship or discipline will I wait

Till my release or graduation cometh.

Thou wilt call (me up into thy presence), and I will answer thee (and come).

Thou wouldst have a desire to (me), the work of Thy (own) Hand.

But *now* (during this time of discipline on earth) thou numberest (or keepest a sharp count on) my steps."

[1] Job xiv. 7-12.
[2] Job xiv. 13-17.
[3] As in Psalm xxvii. 5. "He will keep me secretly in his pavilion: in the covert of his tent will he hide me."

To one coming afresh to see just what Job is saying, it seems plainly a confession of confidence in the final result when the present distress is past. A slight change in the order of the English would seem fairer to Job's thought: "If a man die, he *shall* live, or live again."

Then a little later, maybe half an hour, the mood of talk changes, and he sees only the one thing. Emphasis of certainty fills all his thought as his voice rings out "I *know* that my *Redeemer* liveth."

A glance over the connection[1] makes it plain that "my Redeemer" is put in contrast with a number of other items, "my brethren," "mine acquaintance," "my kinsfolk," "my familiar friends," "my house," "my maid," "my servant," "my wife," "my children," all these have failed in some way. *But*—my *Redeemer,* ah! I *know* about Him. He is unfailing.

That word "Redeemer" had a strong tender intimacy of meaning to Job and his listeners quite missed by us westerners, far removed from the usages of his people. His redeemer was his "goel," that is, his *nearest kinsman* who, because of the tie of blood between them, would come to his help in any distressing emergency. There was no closer family tie than that of the goel, the vindicator, or blood brother, who stood up in his strength to righten the distress or wrong of his kinsman.[2]

Now this distressed man in the tightest corner

---

[1] Job xix. 13-19, 25.
[2] See Leviticus xxv. 25 and Ruth iii. 9-12, iv. 1, 6, 8 and many kindred passages.

of his life, wealth gone, home, children, standing, reputation, all gone, and almost his life gone, at bay before these teasing, nagging pretender friends, cries out: ah! I have a kinsman. He is of my own family and I am of His.

There's the tie of blood between us. He is full able to cover all my need, and He *will* do it. He is my kinsman-redeemer. He will buy back all I've lost, and make it good to me.

"He *liveth*." I don't see Him with these eyes, nor feel Him, nor hear His voice, but He *liveth*. Liveth, a perpetual present tense. I shall know death, but He knows only life. And He is my nearest Kinsman-redeemer. He will see that this death distress is overcome, and I shall live with Him, my Kinsman.

He shall *"stand up"* ready for action on my behalf, when action time comes. "At last," at the end of this troubled earth experience, He will stand up on behalf of me, His kinsman. Death will have done its work. It will have done its worst.

This body of mine itched and tantalized, scratched and weak, shall be laid away with its mother-dust. But that's as far as death can go. It's the last of things here, but the first of things there. Life will just be beginning then.

Then apart from my flesh, separate from it, *I* shall see my Kinsman-redeemer, God, *I*, even *I* myself shall see Him. And He will not be a stranger to me, but my nearest and dearest Kinsman.[1]

[1] Job xix. 25-27 paraphrased, see revision, margin. See paragraph in Preface on paraphrases.

Now note the truth taught. There is continuation of life beyond the grave for this man who is in touch of heart with God. It is in the presence of God Himself, who is known as an intimate friend and kinsman, so it's a joyous life, with all hopes fulfilled. There is continuation of personal identity. "*I* even *I*."

There is a righting of all the unevennesses and wrongs of earth. And the quality of life beyond is the same as God's own life, for He and His redeemed ones are of the same family stock. They are kinsmen. There's no closer tie than the family tie.

It is striking that back in the dawn light of the race this bit of clear teaching stands out so sharp and positive. Even the Fifteenth of First Corinthians is no more positive than this.

Other Old Testament Bits

Much later comes a striking bit in King Saul's time.[1] It is the famous story of the witch of Endor. This story will be taken up fully in the chapter on communication with the dead. It is one of the two exceptional instances in the Bible of communication with those who had died.

Just now we want merely to notice that Samuel did come, to the witch's intense fright and utter astonishment. And, of course, quite apart from her witchery and pretended power. Samuel had been dead for some time. Now he comes back for a brief moment. He was recognized by Saul. He talked just as he had always talked

[1] 1 Samuel xxviii. 3-19.

to Saul before his death. Saul was quick and keen to note that he was getting another stinging rebuke as of old.

Samuel gave precise unmistakeable accurate information of what would happen on the morrow. There is no double-meaninged cryptic playing with words. The kingdom lost to Saul, his defeat in battle, and his death with that of his sons—that's the unwelcome message.

Not only was Samuel still living in the spirit world, but his identity was unmistakeable. His concern in affairs of the earth was keen, as ever. His characteristics were the same, his mentality as vigorous, and his speech as clear and incisive, as before his death.

When David's child died, he says in answer to his servant's surprise and questions, "I will go to him, but he will not return to me."[1] Here is David's belief in the continued existence of his child after death, the expected reunion with one whom his intense emotional nature loved dearly, with identity and recognition both directly implied.

And further there is no hint of any earlier alleviation of their separation through communication with his child during his own life time, though that sort of pretension was the common practice among all the surrounding nations, and well known among the Israelites. Instead it is plainly said that the child would not return to him here.

David's teaching in the Psalms is as clear, and has a running joyous note in it. The Sixteenth

[1] 2 Samuel xii. 23.

Psalm is exultant in its assurance of faith in God, and of God's faithfulness. It makes a running summary of the wondrous blessings in *the present life* of trusting God wholly. And then comes this climax.[1]

"(Even) my body also shall lie down in the grave in confidence.
For thou wilt not abandon, or forsake, my soul in the world of departed spirits;
Neither wilt thou suffer thy holy one himself (thy beloved) to see (or go down into) the pit.
(Instead) thou, personally, wilt show me the path of *life* (while my body waits in confidence the day of reunion):
In thy presence is fulness of joy;
At thy right hand there are pleasures forevermore."

This nut is as full of meat as it can stick. Here is continuation of life after his body has been laid in the grave. It is in the very presence of God, and is a life of fullest pleasure and enjoyment. Clearly, to David's thought, things have reached a climax of joyous living in the life beyond.

He is not less than when here, but more, a wondrous gracious delightful more. There is identity and recognition clearly inferred, and a fulfilment of all he had hoped for. And the resurrection of his body is anticipated, for it lies

[1] Psalm xvi. 9 (second clause)—11, paraphrased.

down in the grave confidently, in hope of a coming day of reunion with his spirit.

The Seventeenth Psalm has the same high exultant assurance. David has been talking of the selfish wicked who oppress him, and who have all their good things in the present life. Then comes this closing bit:

"As for me (in contrast with these others) I shall *behold thy face* in righteousness.
I shall be satisfied, when I awake, with what I find thee to be when I am in thy presence."[1]

Here are the same notes. There is an after life. For himself it will be in God's own presence. It fully satisfies the hopes and expectations even of David's vivid imagination.

The Forty-ninth Psalm, from one of the sons of Korah, runs out in much detail the contrasted conditions between those in touch of heart with God and those not. It's a graphic picture throughout. Then this is placed in sharpest contrast:

"But God will redeem or vindicate my soul from the power of the world of departed spirits (at death). That power will not get control over me.

For *He* (Himself) will *receive* me."[2]

The Seventy-third Psalm, from Asaph's pen, is in the same strain[3] of contrast between

[1] Psalm xvii. 15 paraphrased.
[2] Psalm xlix. 15 paraphrased.
[3] Psalm lxxiii. 24.

the wicked and those trusting God. This is the setting of the words:

"Thou wilt guide *me* with thy counsel (in the midst of the present difficult struggle),

And *afterward* receive me to glory or with glory." And the same contrast comes again later.[1] "The upright shall dwell *in thy presence*," while the wicked are cast into the fire.

Ecclesiastes strikes the low level ideally or spiritually of Solomon's writings. He writes as a jaded cynic, worn dull with his excessive passionate indulgences. But even here is the incidental recognition of the after life. "Who knoweth (any longer here on earth) the spirit of man that goeth *upward,* and the spirit of the beast that goeth *downward.*"[2]

That is, they are both alike *so far as the earth goes*: both gone: both die. The only difference is afterwards, one goes *up,* the other *down.* And again "the dust (of the body) returns to the dust of the earth as it (originally) was, and *the spirit returneth to God who gave it.*"[3]

In an exultant climax of victory over all Israel's enemies, Isaiah cries out, "He hath swallowed up death forever; and the Lord God will wipe away tears from off all faces."[4] This looks forward, is its face meaning, to the coming kingdom on the earth.

But it is also a distinct recognition of the transient character of death. Death is to be

[1] Psalm cxl. 13.
[2] Ecclesiastes iii. 21.
[3] Ecclesiastes xii. 7.
[4] Isaiah xxv. 8.

put to death. And life is to reign in place of death. This passage becomes the more significant as later it is made the basis of Paul's ringing cry of triumph over death in his first Corinthian letter.[1]

In this same climax there is a still more striking bit from Isaiah's pen. Isaiah is talking to God. He says, *"Thy* dead shall live. My dead bodies shall rise (speaking as the national leader). Awake and sing, ye that dwell in the dust (of the grave); for the dew of God is a life-giving dew, and the earth shall cast forth the dead."[2] *There* is a resurrection of the dead bodies of those in touch with God. That is a recognition that their spirits have been living. Now there is a reunion. And it's a time of joyous singing.

Jesus' Teachings—A Test Case

One of the most positive teachings was given by Jesus in the running fire of dispute with some of the national leaders during the last few weeks.[3] It was in His answer to the prize or pet question of the Sadducees.

The Sadducees were the atheists, the rank materialists, of the Jewish nation. Their chief characteristic was a non-belief in the resurrection. But that is merely made the outstanding feature in their creed of atheistic materialism. Now they make a carefully planned attack upon Jesus. They feel so sure of being able to get Him in a corner that their attack is made in

[1] 1 Corinthians xv. 50-57.
[2] Isaiah xxvi. 19 paraphrased.
[3] Mark xii. 18-27 and parallels.

the open, before the thickening Passover crowds. They had a test case to present. It was clearly their standing illustration. They considered it simply unanswerable.

A man had died leaving his widow childless. In accordance with Jewish custom his brother had married the widow to perpetuate the family line. But he also died, and also, childless, and so in turn, seven brothers, each dying without leaving an heir. Now in the resurrection that Jesus believed in and taught, whose wife would she be, for they each had her in turn.

And one can see them chuckling under their breath, with an unholy hate and glee mingling in their gloating eyes. This had never been answered yet. It was unanswerable, they were quite sure. Ah, now they had Him! And out in the open too. It would be a public defeat for this man they hated.

Jesus' reply is so simple and quiet and clear and absolutely convincing that His questioners are utterly silenced. They have no reply. And that is saying a lot for an Oriental, and a Jew, and a Sadducee, and a skeptic.

Jesus answers in effect: "It's no wonder you make such blunders, for you evidently don't know your own Scriptures. And you don't know the power of God. For the other world has not the same limitations as this. There they neither marry nor are given in marriage, but are upon the level of the angels. For *neither can they die any more.*"

Then He goes on in quaint language: "as *touching the dead,* that they are raised; have ye not read in the book of Moses, in the place concerning the Bush, how God spoke unto him saying, 'I am the God of Abraham and the God of Isaac, and the God of Jacob'." Then He adds with that convincing unanswerable quietness: "He is not the God of the dead, but of the living."

God is a God of life. Abraham and these others were indeed dead in the common language and experience of earth; but they were not really dead. They were living when the word was spoken to Moses out of the burning unburnt bush four centuries and more after their death on the earth.

They were living as Jesus spoke the words. They were living with God. They had the same quality as He of being alive. Those in touch of heart with God have the same qualities as He. *All* continue to have some part of creative life. These have the same sort of full life as God Himself. He is a living God. They are living too, the same quality of life as He.

And the force of the answer is seen in the attitude of these critical quizzers. They are silenced, actually silenced! They haven't a word in reply There's a touch of the real in Jesus' words that gives a peculiarly convincing power to them. The Sadducees retire abashed, confounded, dumbfounded, utterly routed. It's such a victory for Jesus that another group of His enemies muster their forces to try to gain some of the lost ground.

God is a living God. Those in touch of heart with Him are like Him. They take on His quality of life. Though they have died here yet they are living. They are living with Him. They are living His sort of life. It's His power that makes it so, overcoming all the power of death. The Book clearly teaches it. So Jesus teaches here.

The Betrayal-Night Talk

The Betrayal-night talk, between Jesus and the inner circle, has some clear explicit bits.[1] Jesus' intimate, John, says plainly that Jesus knew that the time had now come for him to leave this world and *go back up home to the father*.[2]

After Judas has gone out, in spite of the utmost to keep him in, Jesus talks about *His Father's house,* evidently up in another world. He was going there now soon. But in this going away from them He was thinking and planning about them. He was going on their behalf. He was going so as to get a place ready for them to come to.

Then He would come back and take them up with Himself. And so they would all be together again up in the Father's house, gathered about the old home fireside. Could there be a simpler, more realistic picture of life after death, the real life after the abnormal break of death?[3]

Then when things aren't quite plain to their groping minds he goes on to explain that He's

[1] John, chapters xiii-xvii.
[2] John xiii. 1.
[3] John xiv. 1-3.

made an arrangement for the in-between time before this plan had worked out. He would send some One else, like Himself, who would come and stay with them. And He, this coming One, would be everything He Himself had been to them, and immensely more. It is striking that the Holy Spirit here in us, and with us, is clearest evidence about this whole question we are talking over.[1]

That quiet peace in your heart, that hunger to be pure, that prayer tug, all this sort of thing tells of the Spirit's presence within. And it tells too, that that loved one gone from us here, is now up in His presence, face to face, in full enjoyment of the real, griefless life up there.

And then the great simple talk with the Father under the full mellow moon — could any thing make the other world, the reality of the Father, and of things up there, could any thing make these stand out more realistically and dramatically, and satisfyingly?[2]

The words to *the poor thief,* hanging by Jesus' side on Calvary, must have come with a peculiar comfort to that man.[3] *"To-day, thou shalt be with me* in Paradise." The word Paradise clearly stands for some desirable blissful place. Jesus Himself would go there at His death.

He would go there *at once* on leaving the earth. The thief would be *with Him.* They would be alive, and together in this place of enjoyment. This man would be with Jesus *be-*

---

[1] John xiv. 16-26.
[2] John xvii.
[3] Luke xxiii. 39-43.

cause of his attitude toward Jesus, his touch of heart with Him.

That attitude was one of recognition of Jesus as "Lord." There was acceptance of Him as Master. This was a radical change from his early life. It was a penitential change. The prayerful mood was in control now. And there was positive certainty that it would be so—"thou *shalt.*"

The Love Chapter of First Corinthians has a bit of contrast between our understanding of things now, and as it will be at some future time.[1] There is a time coming when prophecy shall be done away, for it will all have been fulfilled; speaking in various tongues shall cease, for there will be one tongue common to all; and the painful acquiring of knowledge shall be a thing past because we shall know fully, and learn easily.

At present we see as something is reflected in a piece of polished steel, or in a mirror, indistinctly, as though through a cloud. But then face-to-face, that is my face, your face, to Jesus' face.[2] Now we know only in part; but then we shall know fully even as now we are fully known. When that which is perfect is come that which is in part shall be done away, or swallowed up, the less in the greater, the thin line of light in the noon shining.

Jesus' Resurrection—Incidentals

That great resurrection climax of Paul's in his letter to his Corinthian converts and friends is

[1] 1 Cor. xiii. 9-12 paraphrased.
[2] Compare Exodus xxxiii. 11.

one of the choice classics of this sacred Book. The whole story there is one of the most fascinating from the Tarsan's thoughtful pen.

The resurrection of Jesus is the chief cornerstone of the whole fabric of Christian truth and fact. But we are not concerned just now with that. But with the other things, the incidentals, tremendous incidentals, that are part and parcel of the other.

Look at these incidentals. There is another world, a spirit world. Jesus is alive up there. He is in command up there. He has at his disposal all things in heaven and on earth. His power is more than we can take in. He is the same Jesus who fed men down here, and healed, and taught, *and* that died.

That upper spirit world is the big thing in comparison with this old earth. It is the center of things, the center of earth control. All things here are regulated there, even the desperate fight against the revolutionary powers of evil. It's the real world.

Jesus' whole heart and thought is in things down here. He holds as precious to Himself, unspeakably precious, every one who follows Him simply and fully, and so is in touch of heart with Himself. His plans of action center here on earth. There's a waiting time just now. With infinite patience He is letting the great sore problem of evil work itself out on the earth.

But one day He will intervene. Intervention is plainly on the schedule. With most studiously careful regard to every one involved, human being and spirit being, he is holding intervention back. For He is just to all, even to the great evil spirit prince.

But the intervention day is as surely coming as that He died and rose again. In this great Corinthian climax the program of action for the earth is given in broad outline.[1] When the intervention day does come then all of His who have died will rise up out of their graves even as He did. As He comes down toward earth, the spirit magnetism of His presence coming nearer will draw their bodies up into reunion with their glad spirits.

Then follows the new order of things on the earth, His order of things at last. And when the purpose of that is achieved, and all contrary rule and authority is utterly abolished, then the kingdom is turned over to the Father. And the climax of the kingdom is this, that death, man's last enemy, is itself put to death.

There is given here too, what may be called *the personal program* He has arranged for His own trusting ones.[2] It is called a "mystery," that is simply instruction or information for the inner circle. The intervention day will be heralded by the sounding of a trumpet as of a summons to form in rank.

Instantly, quicker than you can blink your eyelid, the bodies lying in the grave of those in touch, will know a new life as their spirits, now in Christ's presence, re-enter their old dwelling places, each spirit to his body. And they will rise

[1] 1 Cor. xv. 22-27.
[2] 1 Cor. xv. 50-57.

up toward their center of spirit gravity, the glorified Jesus.

And all those who are living on the earth, and have that same vital heart touch, will as instantly experience some change in their bodies, making them answer to a pull of gravity upward. Courteously they wait until those who have died have preceded them, and then all together, loved one living joined with loved one who has died, they will be at once in the presence of Jesus.

Christ is called here in regard to His resurrection, "the first-fruits".[1] That is, He becomes the model on which His followers' resurrection will be shaped. He rose. They will rise. His body rose: theirs will be raised. His was a changed body, its limitations gone, and new powers come; so theirs. His identity remained, and he was recognized; so with them.

Joseph's emptied tomb becomes a guarantee of countless other emptied graves. Jesus living up there now becomes a guarantee that these others are living. They share the same sort of life as He, a full abundant victorious over-flowing life. He is the "first fruits."

From Paul's Pen

There is no more exquisitely worded reference to the change from this world to the next than in Paul's Second Corinthian letter.[2] He thinks of the body as a tent easily taken down or shifted. Death is the taking down of the tent. He thinks of Christ's Second Coming as meaning

[1] 1 Cor. xv. 20-23.
[2] 2 Cor. v. 1-8.

for him a new sort of life, swallowing up or absorbing into itself the sort of bodily life he is living here.

Then he thinks of the body as a garment or suit of clothing. Dying is like putting the old suit off. It is in anticipation of something better. There's a new suit of clothes to be put on, a new life immediately following the break of death in the old life. If Christ should come while he is still living then the new suit would be put on *over* the old. The new life would swallow up the old or present life without the break of death.

He has the intensest desire that the great change should come, not by death, but by Christ's return. But whichever way it may turn out for him there would be the same happy result. He would instantly be in Christ's own immediate presence revelling in the wondrous new life. To be present here in his body meant absence from the immediate presence of his Lord. And for his spirit to leave his body meant an instant going into the immediate conscious presence of the Lord he so adored.

In the circular letter Paul sent out to the group of churches centering in Ephesus, he pictures the Christ of Gethsemane and Calvary *now seated* in the upper world at the Father's right hand, in absolute possession of all power, both in the spirit world and on the earth.[1]

There is a companion picture to this in Colossians, the two fitting together. The breadth of view in this double picture is refreshing. The Ephesian bit pictures Christ *after* His errand to

[1] Ephesians i. 20-22.

the earth. In this Colossian bit He is seen *before* the errand to the earth.[1]

His presence on earth is like a hyphen, a tremendous tragic glorious hyphen, in His whole career. He it was who did things that far off creative week. Then He did His errand to earth. Then He went back again, and sits quietly waiting the next step in the program that shall show the full roundness of his planning.

There's a bit in the First Thessalonian letter of peculiar interest, because Paul is writing to comfort some who are sorrowing over the death of loved ones.[2] The teaching is tied up with the expected Second Coming of Christ, whenever that may be. As surely as Jesus died and rose again, so sure is it, Paul says, that through Jesus, God will bring up out of the grave into His own presence, *with* Jesus, those trusting ones who have died.

Then he gives the detail of how it will be done. The Lord will descend out of the upper spirit world, where He is now. First of all, those trusting Him will rise up out of their graves; then the living ones who trust are also caught up. And so they are all together. Apart from Second Coming teaching, it is a very real picture of life after death, a glad joyous picture.

The writer of the Hebrews, quite probably some close friend and disciple of Paul, tells what happened on the other side of that cloud that Luke says served Jesus for transit up through the blue. He *"sat down* (as one whose task for

[1] 1 Col. i. 14-18.
[2] 1 Thess. iv. 13-18.

the present was done) on the right hand (the place of power) of the Majesty on high."[1] Plainly there's something very real the other side of the upper blue, and some One very real, too; and some other ones very really with Him.

Peter's First Epistle has some interesting bits of teaching about this whole question we are considering in these talks. We shall be turning to him later. Just now this fits in here.[2] Speaking of Jesus, he says, "being put to death in the flesh, *but* made alive in the spirit."

That "but" seems to throb with eager life. It's a hinge opening the door into the beyond. Peter is referring to what happened to Jesus at the moment of his death on the cross. As he experienced death in his body he likewise experienced just the reverse in his spirit life.

The two parts of the sentence stand in contrast to each other. The force of the language used implies that as there came a *decrease* of life in the body, to the point of extinction, there came an *increase* of life in the spirit. That is, not merely that his spirit continued to live, but that there was an increase of life, either more or, of a different higher sort, or both of these.

In his First Epistle, John says that we don't know at present just what we shall be in the future life. But we do know that when Christ appears openly before the gaze of men, we who are in touch shall be like *Him,* for *we shall see* Him even as He is.[3]

[1] Hebrews i. 3.
[2] 1 Peter iii. 18.
[3] 1 John iii. 2-3.

The Patmos Book

John's Patmos Book begins with a wondrous look at the glorified Jesus, and then gives four looks into the upper spirit world. In that look at Jesus Himself, as seen glorified, there's the simple striking description of His person which quite overwhelms John. But when Jesus begins to talk it is the same sort of talk John was used to from his Master. The gentle right hand touches him again, and the quieting words come,

"Fear not: I am the First and Last, *and the Living One;* and I *became dead* and behold! *I am alive;* I am alive *endlessly;* and more than that, I have the keys, *the absolute control, of death and of the whole spirit world, where men go at death."*[1] That's pretty clear unmistakeably plain talk about life after death from One whom we are disposed to trust to the last ditch.

Then there are four looks at those who are allied in heart with Jesus. In the first, those who have suffered martyrdom for His sake are seen in His own immediate presence, honored and comforted, and told to be patient a bit longer while things are working out on the earth up to the great climax.[2]

In the second look, there's a vast uncountable number who have been caught up out of the great tribulation. They have been purified by the blood of Jesus. Now they are in the immediate presence of the glorified Jesus, singing

---
[1] Rev. i. 17-18 paraphrased.
[2] Rev. vi. 9-11.

rapturously, with shining faces and every mark of delight and victory and fullness of life.[1] They're busily occupied in service, doing the errands and tasks assigned them, and on terms of closest intimacy with Jesus Himself.

The third of these gives the same sort of description.[2] The completed number of the redeemed are in the very presence of the Lord Jesus, singing the wondrous song of the redeemed, purified now, and in fullest fellowship with their Lord, whom they follow absolutely without question or quibble.

Then the last of these looks up into the real world, the headquarters world, comes at the last. All the church has come to love that closing bit of John's Revelation for the winsomeness of the picture drawn. John's own spirit is so stirred in this last book that his grammar has a hard time.

His native Hebrew spirit and thought have a hard time of it trying to tell out the full story in the Greek language which most of the Church he is writing to used. He actually makes new grammatical adjustments. When we see Jesus' face there'll be a good many adjustments, some of them pretty radical ones, too.

Here he sees men of the earth gathered about the Father, as a great family gathers in the evening of a long day about the fireplace in the old home.[3] God and men are living together. Death is gone. Tears and pain are only a memory;

[1] Rev. vii. 9-17.
[2] Rev. xiv. 1-5.
[3] Rev. xxi. 3-7.

There is the sweetest intimacy between God and men, as between a father and his dear son.

Then the scene shifts out to the garden of the home.[1] Here again they are all together in fine fellowship. Men are face-to-face with their wondrous Father-Mother-Saviour God. They are busily occupied with glad errands and tasks at His bidding. Sin's curse is gone. Sickness is no more. Healing is everywhere. It's one long glad daytime, in the gracious sunshine of Jesus' own presence.

An Underscoring of Facts

Now there's an underscoring for all this clear positive teaching. It's a tremendous underscoring. There are in this old Book of God *certain outstanding events* that are illustrations of this teaching. Illustration is the very life-blood of teaching.

One man actually going up off the earth before the watching eyes of men is worth a hundred statements that the thing can be done. One man actually dead and buried, and then rising up out of the grave, where they buried him, and being seen and touched and talked with, this is simply unanswerable.

When teaching is backed up by an event of that sort every doubting critical mouth is shut. The teaching itself stands out in its strength in the presence of the event. The event is explained clearly and fully by the teaching. The two interlace unbreakably. The case could not be stronger.

[1] Rev. xxii. 1-5.

Now, there are in this solitary old Book *twelve separate occurrences,* fully vouched for, illustrating the teaching we have been gathering up. Five of these are in the Old Testament; seven are in the New.

In the Old, there are two men who went up into the other world, the upper spirit world, without dying, Enoch and Elijah. There are two other persons who had died and were then brought back to life, one through the prayer and faith of Elijah, the other through Elisha. And then there's the obscure instance of an unknown man brought back to life through touch with Elisha.

In the New there are three brought back to life through Jesus' power; that is, Jairus' daughter, the son of the widow of Nain, and Lazarus. There is the woman Dorcas of Joppa on the Mediterranean coast, brought back through Peter's action; and the unnamed young man of Troas on the Dardanelles coast, through Paul's intervention.

Then there is the appearance of Moses and Elijah on the Mount of Transfiguration. And at the climax stands the resurrection of Jesus Himself and His ascension, a twin event. Let us look a little at these, briefly, yet enough to make the essential facts stand out clear and distinct.

It is put down as a fact that Enoch went up from earth into God's immediate presence.[1] He did not die. His body was not laid in a grave. He went up body and all, up through

[1] Genesis v. 21-24, with Hebrews xi. 5.

the blue above, into the spirit world where God's own home is. That is the simple tremendous thing put on record here as a fact.

Enoch was not an obscure person. He was the best known man of his day. He was the head of the first family of his time, and the head of the race which was then simply one large family. The outstanding thing in his character, commonly spoken of, was this, in the simple language of the record, that he "walked with God."

And this is directly connected with the unusual manner of his leaving the earth. God and he were on the friendliest terms. It was the realest sort of touch of heart, a true friendship. One can imagine what a sensation the occurrence made. It will be helpful to try to think back and call to mind what effect such an occurrence had *at the time*.

It may have been one day as he was standing in a group on the street of the village, perhaps talking of the reality of God and of God's presence, while some looked askance at him, some were critical, some maybe with an expression of pity that this man, their most famous kinsman, was so *peculiar* on this subject.

While they were looking they are astounded to see his face turn up as though seeing something they couldn't see. A light of rarest beauty overspread his face as though he were looking into the face of his dear Friend. A hush comes over them. Then his feet are off the ground. He's rising up into the air, unsupported by anything they can see; yet he doesn't fall.

He keeps moving up and up, and then is seen

no more. And they know in their inmost spirits, this critical worldly-minded group, they recognize unmistakeably what has happened. God has taken their kinsman up to live with himself in the upper spirit world.

It was a common fact that a man whom everybody knew had disappeared up through the upper blue, and never came back. And furthermore that the strange happening fitted perfectly into this man's desire. His life made it seem a natural thing. As he had walked with God in spirit in his common life it fitted in that he should actually go up and walk with Him in the real world, in the spirit world.

It is vouched for as a fact by this old Book of God. One fact vouches for another. The thing was the talk of the whole racial community. It was not done in a corner. It made Enoch's witnessing tremendous. Without doubt it made a profound impression on the whole race. God was brought into life in a strangely new and very real way.

There seems to have been a purpose of God in this. The occurrence is exceptional. Some day we shall probably understand that better. This man Enoch was peculiarly God's *witness* to the whole race, God's loving faithful witness, when it wasn't easy. He told what he *wot*, what he *wit*, what he *wit*nessed, what he *knew*, about the real God and His friendship with himself. We may hear from Enoch again before things get to their climax. There was a purpose of God in the happening.[1]

[1] Jude verses 4-5.

The Chariots of the Skies

More than twenty centuries after Enoch, a similar event is recorded of another man who was in unusual touch with God, Elijah. He went up while Elisha was watching, up into the air through the blue vault above, body and all. The fact is attested in this Book of God, by a most reputable witness.[1] His going is described in some detail. It is certainly dramatic. In a whirl of wind chariots of flame swept down from above and caught him up and away out of sight.

Elijah is one of the chief outstanding characters of this Book of God. He was a great leader of righteousness. He braved the licentiously idolatrous Ahab in his palace with severest denunciation of his damnable, evil practices. He locked up the windows of heaven for forty-two months, and then unlocked them in most dramatic fashion.

It was said by the last of the Hebrew prophets, Malachi, that he would return for a further bit of outstanding witnessing. This so took hold of the Hebrew imagination that they freely discussed whether Jesus was not Elijah returning as foretold.

John the Herald is said by Jesus, to have fulfilled at that time the ministry spoken of by Elijah. There is good reason for thinking it quite likely that, like Enoch, Elijah's earthly task is not yet done. Each man in his generation was distinctly the outstanding witness to

---

[1] 2 Kings ii. 1-12.

God and God's truth, when belief in both was peculiarly imperilled.

It seems quite likely that the exceptional experience of those two men in their manner of leaving the earth points to a future bit of service down here in some great moral emergency. It was not a reward simply, though that element may have entered in incidentally. It points rather to the future when there will be exceptional need for their exceptional service for God to the race. Apparently they will yet know death.

But just now the bit to mark is that this dependable old Book states as facts that they went up, bodily, into the upper spirit world. So there *is* such a world. Their bodies went up there. Their bodies must have known some radical change fitting them for the new wholly different sphere.

And, as we shall see now in a moment, Elijah clearly retained his identity, and his grade of intelligence up in that spirit realm, not to say any more just now. And whatever would be true of the one, Elijah, would as likely be as true of the other, Enoch.

There are three instances recorded of dead persons being restored to life by Jesus. They are recorded as well authenticated facts. Their significance in this present connection becomes very marked. The three were at different stages of death. Jairus' daughter had just died.[1] The son of the widow of Nain was being carried out

[1] Luke viii. 41-42, 49-56, and parallels.

to his burial.[1] Lazarus had lain in the grave four days.[2]

The fact of death was quite clearly established in each instance. There could be no question in the case of Lazarus, nor of the Nain young man. And when Jesus said to the group in Jairus' house that she was not dead, but asleep, they laughed him to scorn, *"knowing that she was dead."*

That is, all the usual evidences of death in each case were so plain that the thing was beyond question. Their spirits were brought back to the bodies they had left. And the bodies themselves were retouched with vigor so as to serve as a dwellingplace for their spirits. Their spirits were still living while their bodies lay dead. They were recalled from where they were.

So there was not only continuation of spirit life, but identification of the human spirit and its body. Each spirit and its body belong together. Indeed we know that the body comes to take on the character of the human spirit living in it. It is chiefly noticeable to us in the face because that can be read more easily. But the impress of the spirit is in the entire body.

Some other human spirit didn't come back to Lazarus' body. Lazarus' returning spirit did not get into some other body in that graveyard. There was clear identification of spirit and body. When they had that glad reunion supper in Bethany with Jesus as the guest of honor, there was

[1] Luke vii. 11-17.
[2] John xi. 17-44.

no question in anybody's mind about either the identity of Lazarus, or of their recognizing him and he them. Ask Mary what her plain senses told her.

The Transfiguration

We turn now to the story of the transfiguration of Jesus. And we are not concerned just now with its significance. We simply take note of certain incidental facts in the account.

It is put down as a fact that Moses and Elijah were there. Moses had died, something like fifteen hundred years before. Elijah had not died but had disappeared from human view, upward, through the upper blue, something like eight hundred years before. Now both men are plainly seen. Then it is clear that they had been living all that time somewhere else than on the earth.

Their identity was quite clear. The three disciples recognized them at once to be Moses and Elijah. It seems quite unnecessary to say that of course Moses and Elijah recognized each other. They were in closest sympathetic touch with Jesus, His purposes and plans. They knew beforehand what would happen to Jesus at Jerusalem.

There was perfect repose of spirit on their part; no distress, no agonizing. They were perfectly at themselves. Their intelligence was fully on the level they had known and shown in their early lives. Their grasp of the great events being worked out by Jesus' errand to the earth, seems quite full and complete. That is, their outlook takes in events of earth, their connection with the upper world, and it takes in future events.

Clearly they were in full touch of understanding with the great purpose of Christ in going to Calvary, though nobody on earth seemed to understand. They saw things on earth *from God's point of view*. And they recognized that His plans would triumph. They talk of the decease that Jesus would *"accomplish"*.

When the conversation was over they disappeared as they had come. Where did they go? Presumably back up where they had been. By mere inference where are they now? Clearly still living in full possession of their faculties, up in that spirit world where Christ joined them at His ascension.

And it would seem from other scripture[1] that Elijah has a bit of work to do down on the earth before things get straightened out down here. And that it will be the same sort of thing he did so boldly in Ahab's iniquitous day. He seems reserved for that sort of work, and that sort of time.

Evidently these two men are more, than when they were on earth. There is broader grasp, keener spirit perception, and clear knowledge of the way things will work out. Elijah has no use now for that coniferous juniper tree. He has been graduated from the juniper-tree course.

The two instances of Dorcas,[2] and of the

[1] Malachi iv. 5-6.
[2] Acts ix. 36-43.

young man at Troas,[1] give the same essential facts. They add *emphasis* to the others. Tremendous emphasis it is. This is indeed living testimony, irrefutable.

The resurrection of Jesus stands wholly by itself. The fact of His actual death stands indisputable. At the core that's a physician's question. And the simple unlabored use of exact language gives the physician the essential information. The spear thrust into His side brought out, not blood, but "blood and water." The separation in the fluid had taken place. That at once told that death had occurred.

I have no thought of gathering up here the detailed evidences of Jesus' resurrection. There is no point in repeating that. Many excellent summaries can be found in any good library or minister's study. Let it be enough just now to say this, with thoughtful measured words. *There is no fact of common history better authenticated by reliable evidence than the resurrection of Jesus.* This evidential material in the case, considered merely as evidence, is complete and irrefutable. As much can be said for the several appearances of Jesus after the resurrection, and also for His ascension.

This could be called the greatest fact of all. It would be more accurate to say, the fact of greatest significance. Its meaning can be put in this way. Jesus' spirit was living while His body lay in the grave. Then His spirit re-entered His body. Again He moved among men as before, though clearly free of the limitations

[1] Acts xx. 7-12.

known before. He was *recognized*. His *identity* was quite clear. He was *more* afterwards than before. All limitations were gone. A new power lifting Him quite above common conditions was evident.

In plain sight of man He went up, body and all, up through the doorway of the blue above. *He is alive.* He is somewhere *up*. Some day He is coming back, the way He went, He *said*. What has already happened to Him of the sort involved makes it good inferential reasoning that He will do as He has said in this regard. For He is more now than before.

The Damascus Road Event

One other event in this solitary old Book of God crowds for space here. That is the experience of Saul on the Damascus road. It may well be put as a climax to the resurrection of Jesus, for it is a direct result of that resurrection. And a most tremendous result it proves to be.

Saul was a cultured man, of disciplined mentality. In modern language, he was a university-bred man, of an old honored family, and a leader among the younger set in Jerusalem. He was in close touch with the group of Jerusalem leaders that planned the death of Jesus.

He came to the fore shortly after that event, in the persecution of Christ's followers that followed. He became the aggressive leader of this persecution, recognized by the national leaders, and fully empowered by them in his persecuting leadership. He had gone to the extreme degree in hatred of this despised Jesus, and his teachings, and his followers. Nothing could exceed the intensity of his bitter hatred and aggressive persecution. His spirit at this point, is vividly described in the record, "Saul yet breathing threatenings and slaughter against the disciples of the Lord." That is the man Saul.

Then comes the occurrence on the Damascus road.[1] It came suddenly. It became the outstanding experience of Saul's life. He never got over it. Suddenly a light blazed out before his eyes. It came from above. It was not sunlight. It was brighter, this man of keenly trained powers of observation said.

With the strange blaze of light came a power that impelled him, against his will, to fall prone to the earth. There was a clear distinct voice. Then ensued a brief conversation between himself and some One connected with the light and the voice. And this One plainly said, "I am Jesus, whom thou persecutest."

From that hour Saul was an utterly transformed man. From being a bitter enemy, using all his unusual, finely trained, native powers and leadership against Jesus, he became His most devoted follower and exponent. There is no transformation in the character of a strong man so complete, so sudden, and so wide-sweeping. No such similar transformation can be found recorded. Saul's case stands utterly alone, unanswerably alone.

And, mark you keenly, there is no evidence stronger, viewed simply as evidence regardless

[1] Acts ix. 1-22 with parallels.

of moral conclusions involved, none stronger, clearer nor more convincing, evidentially, than the recorded facts in the case of the conversion on the Damascus road of this man Saul, taken in connection with his wide influence in the spread of the Christian faith.

Note the teaching involved. The man Jesus who had been killed was now alive. He was somewhere in an upper spirit world. He was in full possession of His faculties. He was in full vigor of action. He was possessed of a power, clearly more than human, nothing less than superhuman or divine.

His identity, His concern with affairs on the earth, the rare intimacy of His relation with His followers, insisted upon so tenderly and tenaciously, His masterful overwhelming action,—all these were unmistakable to this exceptional, rarely trained, Herculean-willed man, who had so bitterly hated Him. And who now completely reversed his course and became His devoted follower.

Never, was a strong career so radically, so dramatically reversed. His devotion became as marked as his hatred had been. Nothing could dim the burning of his devotion to Jesus. Break of family ties, quite certain loss of family inheritance, break of friendship, the bitterest social ostracism, relentless persecution, truly Oriental in its hounding intensity, the extremest personal hardship continued through years, and at the end a violent death,—all these proved simply fuel to increase the flaming fire of his devotion to the Man of Light and Power and of the Voice, on the Damascus Road.

Such are the teachings, such the events or occurrences, out of which grows the sweet story of assurance regarding loved ones in touch with God, gone from our clinging hungry grasp.

In Touch of Heart

But who are these of whose happy condition in the spirit world we are so sure, and of which we know so much certainly? *All* who have gone? It pains one to say an emphatic no to that question.

I have said it is those *in touch of heart with God*. I have not used that good Bible word, "believe". The two phrases, "in touch of heart with God," and "believing on the Lord Jesus," really mean just the same thing. Then, why not use this last common Bible phrase?

I'll tell you why. "Believe" has been twisted so much out of its simple fine true meaning. It has been made to mean believing *things,* believing creeds and church formulas, and so on. It really does mean just what I have used here. It means *touch of heart with God*. And that touch can be only through Jesus Christ.

That simple language includes a changed attitude toward God where the life has been wrong. It means all that believe, and trust, love and devotion, can mean. There must be the *real personal touch of heart* with our Father-God, who is known only to anyone anywhere through Jesus Christ, the Man who died on Calvary.

I have not spoken of Church membership. Simply because it, too, is another of the fine things that has suffered at men's hands. It has been severely discounted. The true thing is really at a premium. It is to be feared that there are those in church membership who are not in touch of heart with Jesus, God to us. And it is quite clear that there are many not in church membership, many who have no opportunity for that fine privilege, who yet are in the real touch of heart that is the decisive thing.

And I have not spoken of when they have come into that saving touch. With some it may have been a life-long experience; with some a much shorter story. Some come creeping in at close of the day of life, as a tired child creeps into the mother's lap and snuggles down contentedly.

The mother would not turn away her child. And certainly the Man who died will not turn away any that really in heart turn to Him with as much as half the blinking of an eager asking eye.

There will be distinctions made up there, as we have seen, intelligent thoughtful distinctions. But anyone who comes for that touch of heart, however inarticulately expressed, will find himself in the blest presence of Christ at the close of his day of earthly life. And where believing prayer has been sent up for loved ones, there *will* be that touch *some time*. Of that there can be *no question*.

Because of Jesus' Blood

But one last word crowds for place. And I am giving it the most prominent place, at the close, the climax, of this simple heart-to-heart talk. It is this: *Why* are these in the glad conscious presence of Christ and of their loved ones in the upper home-land. *How* do they get there?

And the answer is simple, but it goes to the very tap-root of all Christian teaching. *It is because Jesus died and rose again.* That, all of that, only that, and that to the exclusion of everything else.

There will be no slurring over of sin, nor of stubborn insistence on one's own way in defiance of God's way. Sin can't be ignored, neither by human law, nor by God. Personal rebellion or defiance of God—the very core of sin—can't be slurred over nor winked at.

It will *not* be because we have been consistent members of the Church, nor because active in good works. It will *not* be because of some great personal sacrifice we've made, nor because we've stopped enemy steel and lead with our bodies. It'll *not* even be because we've believed on the Lord Jesus Christ.

It'll be solely and only because Jesus took on Himself what was due us for our sins, and wrong-doing, and the like. His blood poured out till no red drops remained unspilled, His life burned out sacrificially till no white ashes remained for the flames of death to feed upon,—this, only this, is the reason why these go up into yonder Presence.

These other things are good, in so far as they *are* good. Believing is the connecting link with the thing that does the saving. There must be the connecting link, the touch of heart. But the one thing that saves is the precious life-blood of Jesus poured out till death claimed his body. And then His rising again tied the knot on the end of His sacrificial atoning death for us. That made clear and complete His victory over sin and death, and over the prince of death.

A young Italian girl sat at her fruit stand intently absorbed in reading a small book. A gentleman, pausing to get some fruit, asked her what she was reading with so much interest. She replied, rather timidly, "the Word of God, sir."

But he was one who called himself a skeptic, and delighted in spreading his skeptical poison. He said "who told you the Bible is the Word of God?" With child-like simplicity she replied, "God told me, Himself."

"God told you! Impossible! How did He tell you? You have never seen Him nor talked with Him. How could He tell you?" And for a few moments the girl was confused, and silent. Then looking up she said respectfully:

"Sir, who told you there is a sun in the sky up there?" And the gentleman replied, rather contemptuously, "Who told me? Nobody; I don't need to be told. The sun tells this about itself. It warms me. I love its light."

And the young Italian girl earnestly answered, "You have put it straight, sir, for the sun, and for the Bible. That's the way God tells me this is His book. I read it. It warms my heart. It gives me light. I love its light and warmth. None but God could give the light and warmth

I get from this Book." And he turned quietly away, abashed by her simple faith.

I do not know what communion she had connection with. Her nationality would suggest the Latin communion. But there was *the touch of heart with God.*

That's the thing that counts, now and up yonder.

III

THE OTHERS WHO HAVE DIED, WHAT CAN WE CERTAINLY KNOW ABOUT THEM

A Painful Story

There are others who have died. This is a distressing fact, but clearly it is a fact.

This is a painful story. I shall attempt to point out the bad swings of the pendulum, both ways, and then to point out the truth lying in between. It'll be a painful thing to do.

It should be keenly noticed in the start *why* there are others. It is not because of anything that God does. It is because of something that some men do. And it is because, further, of something that they don't do in response to God's repeated wooing. It is by this action, and lack of other sort of action, that *they constitute themselves the others.*

It was clearly never intended that there should be others. It is a break in the original plan. Man has in him the power to break God's plans so far as he himself is concerned. God gave him that power, the highest of all human power, namely, full freedom of choice and decision and action.

There are two fundamental points in the original plan; first, that man should be like God, like Him in fullest freedom of choice and action. And second, that the two, God and man, should always be, and keep, in full touch with each other.

Clearly the second hinged on the first. The full touch could be only through man's choice to have it so. God will not take away that right of free action, even though it be used to break His own heart. He is true to man, and man's highest power, clear to the endless end.

This is a hard story to tell. On one hand to tell it true and straight, and yet not be hard, nor seem hard in the telling. And, on the other hand, to let human feeling have its true full human sway, and yet be true to the man in danger,—it's a hard story to tell. It calls for a rare blend of human feeling and yet of fidelity to facts. One must be both tender *and* true.

It is not at all surprising that the pendulum has had such a time of it swinging back and forth. The common teaching of the Church from, say, the fourth century up to the Protestant revolt was quite definite, with a natural intensifying tendency.

Loyal membership in the Church was taught as essential to salvation from hell. And there was no awed hushing of the voice in pronouncing that fearsome word nor mincing of words nor imagination in picturing its fiery terrors. No account was taken of the vast numbers who had never heard of the Church nor of Christ. One flat statement covered the subject for all.

The Protestant Movement took over the same sweeping positiveness in the teaching on the subject, with one marked outstanding exception. The emphasis on the one essential saving thing was changed from membership in the Church to a saving faith in Christ. But much of the harshness that had characterized the common Church teaching persisted throughout the Protestant Movement, and was quite set in its hardened and ever hardening form. A common reference has been made to a certain well-known French-Swiss leader of the Protestant Movement, picturing infants burning in the flames of the lost world.

Ian Maclaren, in one of his stories of Scotland, pictures a small Scottish lad sitting in the country church listening. It was the evening service. The little church was lit with candles. A candle sputtered on the pulpit desk. The subject of eternal punishment was being discussed. All the boy remembered was the tall lean stern-faced preacher, in silence, holding a piece of paper in the flame of the candle till it was quite consumed, and then in awful tones describing that as what happened to the impenitent.

And the boy, terror-stricken, shrank smaller and tighter into the corner of the hard-seated pew, trying to get away from such a God as was being pictured. That may well be reckoned an extreme instance. We'll hope so. But it points distinctly the general trend.

Bad Pendulum Swings

It was quite the natural thing that there should be a *decided swing away* from such teaching.

The human heart naturally revolted from such a picture. And almost always when the pendulum of teaching starts the other way it goes to the extreme. This swing-away took three forms.

Universalism taught that all men would be saved finally. There would be no others. A proper retribution for wrong would be disciplinary, and corrective. And when the discipline had done its work the man would be saved. By a skillful swinging into view of some Scripture statements, mingled with suitable logic, a strong case is made out, especially for those who want to think that way.

The fair criticism of this teaching is that it takes what statements of scripture suit its purpose, and *ignores* the rest. That's rather a favorite method. Anything can be proven from the Bible by that method. There's another theory that has had wide swing, and has had many exponents. It is called *conditional immortality*. It teaches that only those in touch with Christ have eternal life; the rest simply cease to exist. Annihilationism is another term for the same general teaching.

This is built up chiefly by a skilful playing on the language of Scripture. The plain common meaning of certain words is ignored or slurred over, and the words are restricted to the meaning preferred. Much is made of certain Greek words which are used in the same restricted way as English words.

The bother with this teaching is that it is unphilosophical, illogical, and un-Biblical. It is unphilosophical because *spirit* cannot cease to

Others Who Have Died

exist. It is of the essence of God. It is illogical because it twists and plays with the plain accepted meaning of common language. It is un-Biblical because it plainly ignores certain Scripture statements not suited to its purpose.

A third sort of teaching has had a wide swing. It is called *final restorationism*. It teaches that at some time in the far future, after certain stages of retribution are passed, disciplinary, corrective, and so on, there will be a complete full restoration of all, men, angels and even Satan himself, all restored to perfect touch with God again.

Like the other two, this teaching is based on certain statements of Scripture, certain skilful playing with the meaning of words, certain attractive use of logic, and a careful ignoring of other Scripture statements; a rarely compounded blend of all four of these.

But the commonest idea since the war is what might be called, the *continuance* teaching. That is, there is said to be no real difference, morally or in regard to character, as one crosses the line of death. Death itself, of course, makes a certain radical difference. But apart from that there is no difference, it is said.

The untold thousands who have died in the war, are pictured as wandering about the earth, disembodied, floating through space. They *continue* the old habits of this life, smoking, drinking, using the same sort of profane, and semi-profane and vulgar language. There is no radical moral change, no suffering connected in any way with their former life. And there's **no** change of attitude toward Christ, or good, or sin. This is the commonest teaching of the present day in the vast cheap literature of books and magazines that the crowds are devouring.

Let it be noted carefully that the first and third named are very attractive teachings. A very plausible case can be made in each instance. There is a tremendous emotional appeal in them. One could most earnestly wish that they were full true.

May I say, very reverently, that I have no doubt it is the devout wish of God that they might be true. For anything else is a break in His cherished plans. But they all fail to take account of two fundamental things, man's utter freedom of choice, *and* the real character of the thing commonly called sin.

We all laugh at the ostrich for hiding its small head in the sand so as not to see the danger threatening. Yet to ignore *any facts,* and to ignore plain teaching of God's Word, clearly is as much playing the fool as does the poor small-brained ostrich. One fact, *just one,* left out of reckoning, completely changes the conclusion. Such conclusion, however skilfully and logically worked out, is quite worthless, and worse yet, dangerous, because misleading.

As a result of the wide spread of these and like teachings, there has come a most marked swing away, among adherents of Protestant churches of all shades, from the old teaching. And the loosening hold of the Catholic Church upon its people comes to much the same thing.

The boast of certain so-called liberal denominations is that they have not increased in *numbers,* but that their teachings have permeated all the other Churches. And all observation tends to confirm their contention.

Some War-time Teachings

Without doubt the common feeling to-day in all our churches is that a man will "pull safely through somehow." Regardless of his belief or lack of it, regardless of his manner of life, he will finally get safely past all danger of this thing called punishment or hell; things will go "all right" with him.

Of quite recent years a certain type of evangelist has had a swing throughout our American cities, truly remarkable for some features of such effort. They are widely endorsed as preaching "the old Gospel." Their frequent reference to future punishment has been one of the prominent features.

But blunt plainness of speech has run into a usage of the words "hell" and "damned," and the like, that is such an imitation of common vulgar profanity as to be really blasphemous, and to make one cringe.

And the common attitude of the crowds toward the subject itself is quickly and painfully revealed in the peals of laughter and the applause greeting all such references. It seems plainly a matter of merriment to them, so far has the pendulum swung the other way.

The war has intensified tremendously some good tendencies, and a great many very bad ones. And certainly this matter has not escaped its evil contagion. On both sides the water the teaching has been common that if a soldier made his so-called supreme sacrifice in action, that that would absolutely secure his salvation. This has been repeated so commonly and so positively as to have been accepted by the crowds.

Certainly no loyal Britisher nor American would wish to diminish one whit recognition of the splendid sacrifice made by thousands of soldiers during the war. But it is surely a great unkindness, a grievous wrong, to those men, not to say more just now, so to deceive them, and that on the very edge of possible death.

A minister friend told me of an experience he had. He was visiting one of our great soldier camps. He was trying to tell the real Gospel story, tactfully, winningly and fully. A soldier with serious face came to his quarters one night after service.

He said, "We men have been discussing this thing down our street, and we had it settled that if we die in action, our salvation's secured. That's what we've been told. Now, you say there must be something else to fix things for us. We men are all mixed up." And my friend tried in his brotherly fashion to make things clear.

Recently at an international convention of rescue mission workers, it was the common agreement among the delegates that this idea was so inbred with ex-service men that it immensely hindered efforts to win them to a simple faith in Christ.

Very thoughtfully it can be said that every-

Others Who Have Died 101

where this is the commonplace of belief regarding any such thing as punishment in the after life for wrong doing. It simply isn't so. That's the common thought. It is the extreme swing of the pendulum from the other extreme teaching of the Church in earlier centuries and even recent years.

These are two extremes. At one extreme hell is practically the biggest thing in the universe, with heaven a small affair, comparatively. At the other extreme there is no hell at all. It is quite rubbed out.

You say, "that's putting it too strong isn't it? Hell the biggest thing?" No, that is the simple direct logical conclusion of the common teaching for centuries. Those who have been in the membership of the Church in pre-Protestant days, and the members of the Catholic Church since, are a distinct minority of the whole race, even reckoning, as was done, that all subjects of Catholic countries were, and are, members of the Church. Indeed it would be quite fair to say a *small minority,* as one thinks through the *gradual* spread of Church authority in European lands during early centuries.

And then, recalling the common Protestant qualification for salvation, which, of course, is the Scriptural one, all those who have *heard* of Jesus Christ since He was on earth, in any way, would be a somewhat less-small minority, *and* all who have accepted Him even nominally are a distinctly smaller minority. And beyond that point we won't push just now.

Now, think around the earth, and think

through the long centuries. Quite clearly, according to the *common interpretation* of both qualifications, the vast majority must be reckoned outside, consigned to endless woe. That's the plain logical conclusion. Is it surprising that the swing has been so strong toward the no-hell extreme? We shall find the truth in between these two extremes.

Spirit-Level Accuracy

Now we want to turn to this Book of God. And we want to get *all* of what it says, and fit together in one simple clear story. Clearly this is the only sane thing to do, get *all* the Book says, take its statements at their plain common meaning, and let that tell the story, *regardless* of how it may send our theories and ideas helter-skelter. Any thing else is clearly a fool's job.

Have you ever watched a skilful bricklayer at work He has a delicately constructed instrument called a *spirit-level*. The instrument is so constructed as to indicate if a surface is quite level, or, is out of the level. As the brick-mason lays his bricks, layer-by-layer, he is constantly holding the spirit-level to the work to test its being level or straight.

He puts it on top of the bricks, and in front, and up and down, constantly testing. He would tell you it's the only safe thing to do. All surveyors and builders use such a device, a standard gauge for determining levels accurately. They must. They have no choice. Otherwise they and their work would be rejected.

Others Who Have Died 103

Recently I watched a sort of scrub bricklayer at work on the foundation of a small frame house that had been moved. He had no spirit-level. He went "by his eye." That was quite satisfactory to him. But the work he did was anything but satisfactory. It was painfully out of level, though as it happened, in this small unimportant case, apparently, not dangerous.

But as I watched him I thought of other builders, builders of character, who go "by the eye," or by what they prefer to *think* is sufficient standard. And pretty wobbly work they do in character-building. And the bother is, there's serious danger to life, in their inefficient standardless work.

Happily there is a spirit-level by which to test all human teachers and teachings. And there's only one, as with the brick-layer and surveyor. And whatever work is not done by the standard spirit-level, is worthless, and worse yet, may prove very dangerous to human life.

This is a three-part spirit-level: the *Holy Spirit,* in the *Book,* and that in the hands of *a man strongly yielded* to the Spirit's sway. The Spirit Himself is the standard. He speaks in this Book. And so it becomes the standard. And its teachings can be fully and clearly grasped only by one in touch with that Spirit, naturally. Though any one may read and get the general drift of teaching.

And so, now, we want to turn and try to find out just what the teaching of this Book is, the rounded-out, poised, full, teaching, on this most vital subject. This talk and the last one of this series, "Another Chance," belong together. They touch two phases.

They are put separately as a matter of teaching principle, to get a clearer look at each phase and so a clearer grasp of the whole thing. This talk gathers up the *facts* in the case. The last talk touches the *principle* and *process* underlying the facts.

Truth Makes a Clean Cut

Turning now to the Book, the first thing one notes is this, there is a sharp distinction drawn between those not in touch of heart with God, commonly called here "the wicked," and those in touch of heart with Him, commonlly called here "the righteous." In these talks these two alternate phrases are taken as exact equivalents. That sharp distinction is markedly prominent in the Psalms, and the Gospels, but indeed runs clear through, from end to end, of the Book. There is none of the slurring over so familiar among us today.

A second thing that stands out clean-cut and sharp is this, that distinction plainly extends beyond the line of death. The same moral differences noted in this life persist beyond the grave. I had almost said that it is on every page, so common is it. These are two most striking things to note at the outstart. The spirit-level marks a difference at once, and a persistent difference.

Now, note the language used in the Old Testament for the place where the wicked dead are said to go. For instance, "Jehovah hath executed judgment; the wicked is snared in the work of his own hands. The wicked shall be turned into hell, even all the peoples that forget God."[1]

The Hebrew word under that English word "hell" is "sheol," so translated literally in the revised versions. The word "sheol" itself means literally, the underworld, a cavity, or a hollow subterranean place. It has two distinct meanings in the common usage of the Bible times, a neutral meaning, and a positive meaning.

In its neutral meaning it refers simply to the world of departed human spirits, regardless of what their condition there is. In its positive meaning it is used for the place of punishment. The wicked are spoken of as having gone to "Sheol," but they are *not* in God's presence, but instead they are said to be in torment and anguish.

Those who have died, being in touch of heart with God, are spoken of as being in sheol (the world of departed spirits), but they are also spoken of as being in the *immediate presence of God*. The word, neutral in itself, gets its positive meaning from some words *added*, to make the meaning quite clear.

For instance, "a fire is kindled in my anger, and burneth unto the lowest hell (sheol)."[2] Here it is associated directly with fire, and with punishment on evil. Speaking warningly of the adulterous woman and those in fellowship with her, "her steps take hold of hell" (sheol); "her

[1] Psalm ix. 16, 17.
[2] Deuteronomy xxxii. 22 see connection.

house is the way to hell" (sheol); "her guests are in the depths of hell" (sheol).[1]

Speaking of the arch-enemy of God and of all good, "hell (sheol) from beneath is moved for thee to meet thee at thy coming." "Thou shalt be brought down to hell" (sheol).[2]

About half the number of times the word is used it is translated "the grave," in the old authorized version; the other half (roughly), "hell"; a few times, "the pit."

In the New Testament there are two Greek words translated, in the common version, "hell". These two are "Hades" and "Gehenna". They cover the same ground as the one word "sheol" in the Old. The word "Hades" is neutral. It means simply the world of departed human spirits, where all go who die.

The other word, "Gehenna," originally was the name for the valley outside Jerusalem where in earlier days little children were thrown into fire in idolatrous worship. When this horrible practice was abolished, the place was used for all sorts of refuse, for dead animals, and the unburied bodies of criminals. Its fires continually burned with an intense burning.

Now this word is clearly used by Christ as a name for the place of punishment for wicked men. For instance Jesus says of certain ones, "shall be in danger of the hell (Gehenna) of fire."[3] Here plainly it cannot mean the

[1] Proverbs v. 5; 7; 27; ix. 18.
[2] Isaiah xiv. 9, 15.
[3] Matthew v. 22, 29, 30. See also for usage of Gehenna, Matthew x. 28; xviii. 9; xxiii. 15, 33.

Gehenna burning outside the Jerusalem walls. It must mean something else, something for certain men corresponding to this fire for the refuse.

Then it is noted that toward the close, in the Revelation, other words are used in the same sense as Gehenna is used earlier, "abyss," "the lake of fire," and "the second death". These last two are said to be the same thing.

Thither are said to go, Satan, his human leaders in the last great warfare against God, and all men not in touch of heart with God.[1] There is the distinct intimation that this is the final disposition of these, as though the final permanent form which things take for these mentioned.

Jesus' Plain Teachings

Now turn to *Jesus' own teachings*. Shall we remind ourselves of the outstanding character of Jesus, His humanness, His sympathy with suffering, His tenderness of heart and of speech, His self forgetful unselfishness in relieving suffering? These are among His most characteristic traits, admitted and admired by all. All this makes certain teachings stand out in bold relief.

Look at some of these words of His. "Enter ye in by the narrow gate, for wide is the gate and broad is the way *that leadeth to destruction* . . ." For narrow is the gate and straightened the way that leadeth unto life."[2] Here "destruction" is put in contrast with "life". There

[1] See Revelation xix. 20; xx. 1-3, 6, 10, 14-15.
[2] Matthew vii. 13, 14.

are two ways and two radically different ends to them.

"Many will say to me in that day, Lord, Lord, did we not prophecy in thy name," and so on. "And then will I profess unto them, I never knew you; *depart from me,* ye that *work iniquity.*"[1] Here the absence of touch of heart is hidden under religious pretensions. And the result is put as absence from Christ's presence in the future life.

More vigorous language is used a little later in the same connection, where those not in touch of heart are "cast forth *into the outer darkness;* there shall be the weeping and gnashing of teeth".[2] Unmistakeable talk, that! And under the guise of a parable the same dread language is used twice again for those found lacking in the final settlements.[3]

The fact of a settlement day for all men, with a most studious fairness in taking account of all modifying facts and circumstances, and a dreadful result for some, is plainly taught in these thrice repeated words, "it shall be more tolerable for the land of Sodom and Gomorrah (who were visited even in this life with such terrible judgment) in the day of judgment, than for you."[4]

Listen again: In the end of the (present) age, "the Son of Man shall . . gather out . . all things that cause stumbling, and them that do

[1] Matthew vii. 22, 23.
[2] Matthew viii. 12.
[3] Matthew xxii. 13; xxv. 30.
[4] Matthew x. 15; xi. 22, 24 with variations.

iniquity, and shall cast them into *the furnace of fire*: There shall be the weeping and the gnashing of teeth."[1] Could words be plainer or more heart-breaking?

With a triple variation of language, he says that it is better to suffer some in this life in the decision to be true and keep true than to suffer immeasurably more in the next life. "It is better for thee to enter into life maimed rather than . . to go into the Gehenna, into the unquenchable fire." Then is added the terribly graphic rhetoric "where their worm dieth not, and the fire is not quenched."[2]

In the close of His talk on Mount Olivet, He pictures the adjustments of the final settlement time in terrible language: "Then shall the king (pictured in verse thirty-one as Himself) say unto them on His left hand, depart from me under a *curse* into the *eternal fire*." And, "these shall go away into *eternal* punishment."[3]

And again listen to this word: "He that obeyeth not the Son shall not see life, but *the wrath of God abideth on Him*.[4] With these quotations from Jesus' own lips, can there be any question as to *the impression He meant to give in these teachings?*

A Hard List to Quote

Let me add only a few others to this list of heart-breaking quotations. Paul tells the Athenians, "(God) hath appointed a day in which *He*

[1] Matthew xiii. 41, 42 and repeated with variation in verses 49, 50.
[2] Mark ix. 43-49.
[3] Matthew xxv. 41, 46. [4] John iii. 36.

will judge the world in righteousness by the Man whom He hath appointed."[1]

He speaks plainly in the Romans epistle about the impenitent: "after thy hardness and impenitent heart treasurest up for thyself wrath in *the day of wrath* and revelation of the righteous judgment of God, who will render to every man what is due to his deed. . . unto them who are men of guile, selfishness, cunning, and obey not the truth, but obey unrighteousness, shall be *wrath* and *indignation; tribulation* and *anguish* upon every spirit of man that worketh evil."[2]

"The Lord knoweth how (i. e., fairly in justice) to keep the unrighteous *under punishment,* unto the day of judgment."[3] And this bit, "the heavens that now are, and the earth by the same word (of God as in creation) have been *stored up with fire,* being reserved against the day of judgment and destruction of ungodly men".[4] Jude's intense little letter has this, "angels. . . he hath kept in everlasting bonds under *darkness* unto the judgment of the great day."[5]

It is most striking that in the midst of that final description of rarest beauty of the heavenly world, which has so taken hold of the human heart, right in the very heart of it, in sharpest contrast with all the surroundings, stands this bit: "But the cowards, and unbelieving, and abominable, and murderers, and fornicators, and

[1] Acts xvii. 31.
[2] Romans ii. 5-6, 8-9, paraphrased partly.
[3] 2 Peter ii. 9.
[4] 2 Peter iii. 7 read connection.
[5] Jude vi.

dealers with demons, and worshippers of anything and any one else than God, and all sorts of liars, *their* part shall be in the *lake of fire* and brimstone; which is the *second death*.[1]

And the last word is this: *"without* are the mangy scavenger dogs, and the partners with demons. . . and everyone that doeth a lie."[2] What a world of meaning packed into one word—*"without"*. It stands in contrast with the vision of rare beauty of God's homeland. Could more be said? Could anything be worse? Without!

That ends the list at present. And I am personally glad. It has been a task of suffering to gather them out, and go over them, word by word, and pile them all up together. I'm glad the heart-breaking task is done for now.

It will be noted that there seem to be two stages in point of time, in the place of punishment. At the *present time* these others are somewhere separated from God, and in mental and spirit anguish. The words used are "Gehenna", "outer darkness", "unquenchable fire", and the like.

There seems a second stage indicated, a final stage, called "the lake of fire", and "the second death", which are indicated as the same thing. Satan himself is *now* not in hell, but somewhere in the lower heavens below God's throne, and above the earth.[3] He is to be cast down to the earth, and later is cast into the abyss, or the

---

[1] Revelations xxi. 8 paraphrased.
[2] Revelations xxii. 15 paraphrased partly.
[3] Ephesians vi. 12 l. c. with Revelation xii. 7.

lake of fire.[1] This is the phrase used for the final place for both Satan and some men.

There seems to be a program of events outlined, with which this is connected. There is to be a different order of things on the earth some day, running a long time. At its close there is a short moral crisis on the earth. And then follows the *final disposition* of things. The final settlement with Satan and any preferring Satan's way, comes in this final disposition.

The Meaning of "Torment."

But there is one outstanding bit of Jesus' teaching that deals explicitly with this matter of the life beyond the grave. And I want to bring it in here. It is the remarkable story of the rich man and poor beggar in the Sixteenth of Luke. The story is drawn out by the criticism of the Pharisees, and is aimed directly at them.

The Pharisees were the dominant party in Jewish politics. They were the official religious leaders. For church and state were one thing. They posed before the crowds as saints. And it was notorious that they were as bad in their lives as bad could be. Their criticism of Jesus for His friendliness to the poorest classes drew out the three matchless parables of the Fifteenth of Luke, and that of the unjust steward in the Sixteenth.

The Pharisee leaders were in the crowd listening. The money parable stirred them. They scoffed openly. For they were *"lovers of money."* Then Jesus touched another sorely sensitive spot

[1] Revelation xii. 9; xix. 20; xx. 1-2, 10.

Others Who Have Died

with them by speaking of the easy divorce so common among them.

Then at once He begins on this story of the rich man and the poor beggar. Their conditions *in this life* are touched first. The rich man was not simply rich. He was notoriously selfish. He lived "in mirth and splendour every day," a constant round of lavish selfish pleasure-seeking.

The beggar was afflicted in body as well as being a pauper. He was carried by some kind friend of his class to the rich man's gate daily, depending on scraps for subsistence. But even the dogs were kinder to him than his selfish rich brother-man whose servants threw out the crumbs.

Then there's the swift sudden change. The beggar died. That was the earthly end for him. The rich man died, *and was buried*. The splendour of life lingered over his remains. That was the earthly end for him.

Then comes the second picture, in *the next life*. Again there's the same painful contrast between the two, but with places exactly reversed. The beggar is tenderly carried by angels up into Abraham's bosom, the Jewish statement for utmost bliss. Not because he is a beggar, of course. He simply goes by natural spirit gravity to where his spirit kinsfolk are.

The rich man is in Hades. That tells us nothing of his condition until the phrase is added, "being in *torment*." That last word tells the story for him. It is so not, of course, because he is rich. He simply goes by natural movement to his center of spirit gravity.

That word *"torment"* is the significant word. Let us look at its meaning. It is used four times in this story, in our common authorized version. There are two different words underneath. The Revisions translate one of these, "in anguish." The rich man says, "I am in anguish in this flame." And Abraham says, "thou art in anguish."

This word translated anguish occurs four times in the New Testament. It occurs twice here. It is the word used of Joseph and Mary's distress over the absence of the boy Jesus,[1] and by Paul's Ephesian friends over his farewell words.[2] In both cases it is translated *sorrowing*.

Thayer's Greek Lexicon indicates these as the only occurrences. Its original meaning is to cause intense pain, to be in anguish, to torment or distress one's self. The word clearly refers to one's mental and spirit condition, simply that.

The other word translated here "torment," occurs in varying form twenty-two times, in thirteen instances.[3] It is translated "vexed" once, "pained" or "in pain" once, "distressed" twice, and some form of "torment" eighteen times. Once the alternate phrase "have no rest" is added, and once "sorrow," where torment is used. Its original meaning has reference to the

[1] Luke ii. 48.
[2] Acts xx. 38.
[3] Matthew iv. 24; viii. 6; viii. 29 (Mark v. 7; Luke viii. 28); Matthew xiv. 24; (Mark vi. 48) xviii. 34; Luke xvi. 23, 28; 2 Peter ii. 8; Revelation ix. 5; (three times); xi. 10; xii. 2; xiv. 10-11 (twice); xviii. 7, 10, 15; xx. 10.

testing of metals by a touchstone. It came to be used for testing by torture to compel one to tell the truth. The meaning of all words grows and changes with usage. Note the usage in the Scriptures of this word.

Twice it is used of intense suffering through disease, once for the pains of child-birth, once for the difficulty of rowing in a storm, twice for persons distressed in mind and spirit by the conduct of others, once as a name for a jailor, once by demons of their suffering, once of pain inflicted upon men by demons, once of Satan's suffering in the future state, once of suffering in the future state by men, once of the doom of Babylon, and twice of the suffering of this rich man in the story we are studying. That is to say, omitting the story in Luke, and omitting the use as a name for a jailor, six times it is used for pain or suffering wholly within one's self connected with the common experiences of life, and two of these six times the suffering is wholly of mind and spirit.

Twice it is used of demons suffering. Three times it is used of punishment inflicted in judgment. But whether, in this last the suffering is of mind and spirit only, or through some positive act of God in punishment is not specified. Judging by this usage it would seem usually to mean pain growing out of one's actions or through common experience and not through arbitrarily chosen punishment inflicted by God.

Turning back now to the story of this man, he says, using this word, "I am *in anguish* in this flame." And his pain, as of being burned by fire, is further stressed in this plea to Abraham "that he may dip his finger in water and cool my *tongue.*" The language intimates that it is a terrible thirst that is burning him up.

It will be noticed that there is no change of spirit or of heart in this rich man. The only thing that is bothering him is his suffering. There's no thought of regret nor of remorse for the intense selfishness of his former life. And his plea, while a perfectly natural one, is still simply to get some ease for himself.

He is sorry to be in such an awful fix. There's no suggestion of anything beyond that. Clearly his attitude toward God remains as before. The life there in that regard is merely an extension of the life he lived here. He is the same man in spirit as he was. That's clear, and that seems the decisive thing.

And in Abraham's reply to his plea, two things stand sharply out. There can be no alleviation of pain by the method the rich man suggests.

And the added words take hard hold of one's eye and ear and inner being, "between us and you *there's a great gulf fixed,*" an impassable gulf. What that gulf is will be touched upon in our last talk, on "Another Chance." Just now it's enough to let the terrible fact stand out, naked and gaunt and real.

This is the most outstanding teaching on this matter from the lips of the tender-hearted, tender-spoken Jesus. There's another life beyond the grave. There's a distinction made between men in that next life. That distinction is shaped up, down in this life.

It continues beyond the grave as started here. There is a place of intensest pain of some sort over there. The language used here suggests simply pain of spirit. That of course is the intensest kind known. There's also a place of happiness. Some are in each. There's an impassable gulf between the two.

In Their Own Shoes

Now, let me try to gather up a few conclusions from all these and kindred passages. There is a sharp distinction drawn between two classes of men. It is based wholly on their voluntary continued attitude of heart toward the good and right and pure.

At the present time God is not acting in judgment. He is letting things work out their natural course. But he is keeping close watch, and there's a day of settlement surely coming.

There's a place of punishment in the next life. It passes through two stages. There is the present stage, running concurrently with the history of man on the earth. There is the final stage, beginning with the completely new adjustment of heavens and earth.

That place of punishment is a place of intensest pain of mind and spirit. It is not clear that there is anything in addition to that intensest of all suffering. The inferences are against its being so.

That place is not made by God. It is the creation or product of those who stubbornly set themselves against God. It seems that their accumulated action carried to its logical extent, with an increasing momentum, produces the condition that is called hell. That is the word used for the place where all such will go by the natural movement of their spirit gravity.

God does not send any one there. Whoever goes there, goes on his own feet, in his own shoes, by the use of his own free action and only so. And it seems quite clear that he *stays* there in the same way as he goes.

Hell has, and will have, no such huge population as would be logically concluded from much teaching on the subject. But there is unmistakeable evidence that there is a group of incorrigibles. The language of Scripture leads one to say, a small minority of incorrigibles.

Note these words used at the very close, "and *if any* was not found written in the book of life, he was cast into the lake of fire."[1] Those words "if" and "any" are very suggestive. It is not the language we commonly use for a great crowd, but rather of exceptional instances.

That all this is so is utterly heart-breaking to God. It is wholly against His will and plan. But, with the utmost reverence be it said, that God Himself cannot change the thing without infringing on man's utter freedom of action. The only possible way of removing utterly any even remote possibility of hell would be by destroying man's freedom of action.

It is objected that, if all this be so, it is a defeat for God. And so, it is said it could not be, for surely at the last God will be completely tri-

[1] Revelation xx. 15.

Others Who Have Died

umphant. And that has a very very strong appeal in it.

It is to be noted however, that such reasoning is not based on God's revelation, but on logic, our reasoning processes. Logic is very subtle. The least slip in the process spoils the conclusions. And logic is a very slippery thing. One item left out, even though unconsciously, knocks the conclusion out.

On the other side, there are two things to be said. God *will* be victorious, even under such circumstances as outlined in this talk, in this: He will have held unflinchingly and unfalteringly, to the original high standard for man, namely that man shall be in His own very image. He will have held to it *against* the utmost to swerve Him from it. Man is as free in his will as God is in His.

Man retains his high estate in being free to use his will as he will, even while he is damning himself in using it in a bad way. It is full victory for God's great love-purpose in creation. And meanwhile there is clear inferential evidence that the door of right choice is always open, even though it is never used by some. This is the reasoned-out reply. It is the logic process. And again it is recalled that a single flaw in logical reasoning, even though undiscovered, a single factor omitted, quite changes the conclusion.

There's something better, more conclusive, on the other side. That is the revealed fact of truth in God's inspired Book. A single citation here contains enough if there were no more. It is from the final view given of earth's affairs. It deals with the racial climax. It is the description of God's ideal at the very culmination.[1] Evil has been judged finally.

Satan is disposed of. The old earth is displaced by a new or wholly regenerated earth. Our language seems almost used to the full in the attempt to picture the beauty and bliss, the peace and happiness, of that ideal, now become really real.

In the very midst of this glowing highly-colored picture comes the bit to be quoted here. It could not stand in sharper contrast with its immediate surroundings than it does. It is like a spot of blackest ink on whitest paper, like a mangy cur among thoroughbreds. It's a thing a *man,* of himself, would never have done, put this statement in that setting of bliss and purity and beauty.

Listen to the words so out of keeping with their surroundings:—"But"—*but,* what a tremendous but!—"for the fearful (or cowardly) and abominable, and murderers, and fornicators, and sorcerers (partners with demon spirits) and idolaters (worshippers of anything and any one rather than of God), and all (sorts of) liars, *their* part is in the lake that burneth with fire and brimstone, which is the second death."[2]

That doesn't at all mean that these people are commonly known as murderers and sorcerers and liars and so on. Some of them may be. It is the language of the Holy Spirit. It is de-

[1] Revelation xxi. 1; xxii. 5.
[2] Revelation xxi. 8.

Others Who Have Died 121

scribing things as He sees them.[1] His eye looks through to the motives as well as the common trend of life. Many of these are what would be called cultured persons, moving in church circles.

But the Holy Spirit, looking down into their motives and lives, sees that *this* man is using some power he has against another to the degree of shortening the other's life or worse. *That* man is unclean in his thoughts and imagination and acts. This *other* one is having communication with evil spirits, which is commonly called spiritism; and that one *yonder* is *living* a lie, or practicing deception.

"Without"

And in the epilogue the same note is struck again. And it is most significant that this time it is directly connected with that highest of all human powers, *free choice,* God's best gift to man. Listen: "He that is set on being unrighteous, let him be free to follow his choice and do unrighteousness, and it will be with a constantly increasing momentum.

"And he that is set on going to the passionate depths of evil doing will be free to follow *his* bent, with the slant down getting steeper."[2] And then the same thing, in the same two degrees, is spoken of those choosing the right way.

And when Jesus comes to get things straightened out, He will give to each man as his choice

---

[1] Note the blunt honest language used by the Holy Spirit of the apostle Judas. John xii. 6.
[2] Revelation xxii. 11 paraphrased.

has been.[1] And then blessing is pronounced on those who insist on choosing the right regardless of difficulties and opposition, and so do the thing that goes with right choice, go for cleansing to the Blood of the Lamb.[2]

Then immediately comes the terrible "without" sentence. "Without are those whose choice takes them there, those who do not go to be washed." And the Eye that sees things just as they are, sees that underneath whatever veneering may be used, they are in spirit as the mangy scavenger curs of the Orient, they are those having touch with demon spirits, the unclean, those who unfeelingly use their power to crowd others to the shortening of their lives, those that put self and its interests above God, and the climax is reached in those who love and practice deception of any sort.[3]

Who shall speak after God? Who shall give contrary opinion after the Book has spoken? This is the last word on the subject. And the ostrich shutting its eyes to danger becomes a surer victim of the danger. We'll do well not to see an ostrich if there's a mirror at hand.

That is all for now. We take the matter up again from a totally different angle, in our last Talk. This Talk deals with the *facts* in the case. The last one deals with the *principle* and the *process* that underly and go with the facts.

It's been a hard story to tell. It's been told

[1] Revelation xxii. 12 paraphrased.
[2] Revelation xxii. 14 with vii. 14.
[3] Revelation xxii. 15 paraphrased.

with an aching heart. Yet the truth must be told simply, clearly, and in due connection with related truth. To be tender-hearted without being truthful is not loving. It *is* unkind. It is cowardly.

To tell such truth, without being broken-hearted by the awfulness of it, is to be hard-hearted, inhuman, un-Godlike. Jesus' most terrible denunciation of the Jewish leaders ends in a great sob.[1] And a few days later that sob of grief broke his heart. He made the one great solitary sacrifice, that no man might ever be left outside because of his sin score; that so the man who chooses Him as Saviour may have the full right in the Father's house.

I recall sitting one evening as a guest in the big dining room of the Moody Bible Institute in Chicago. Mr. Moody himself was sitting at the head of the faculty table. And after the meal there was a little informal speaking. A member of the faculty told a witty story, the point of which was regarding future punishment. It was greeted with a general laugh.

Instantly Mr. Moody was on his feet. "Well," he said, "whenever you do talk about hell, *let it be with tears in your voice.*" There was the rare blend of tenderness and truth that always marked Moody, and Moody's Master.

---

[1] Matthew xxiii. 37.

IV

CAN WE HAVE COMMUNICATION WITH THE DEAD?

A True Human Instinct

It is perfectly natural to want to talk with our loved ones who have died. It adds to our grief that we cannot.

It's a true human instinct to miss them, and long intensely for them, and to feel lonely in their absence. All this may be kept out of sight, pretty much, under a strong good self-control. But anything else is not natural.

Death is always a shock, even when expected. It makes a bad break in one's life. I know a young man who wrote to his mother every day, even if only a few lines, when his work took him quite away from her. And when she slipped from his grasp it took the longest time and some strange feelings to break that daily writing habit.

He had prayed daily for her. And it seemed so queer not to. It seemed like not being true to her, as though it were disloyal not to be naming her in the daily prayer. Then he learned to put praise in the place of the old-time prayer, that she was safe past troublous things, up in the Master's own presence. But what a wrench that change of habit did make!

I have a dear friend whose husband suddenly

snapped the life-cord, and was gone. They had lived an ideal life together for long years. She always leaned upon his counsel and fellowship in family matters. And it seemed as if she *could* not get used to doing without him. A bit of her very self had gone.

Grief, tense, deep, overwhelming, is the natural thing. Its emotional sweep and suction is tremendous, quite beyond words. It takes a fine strong self-control to hold steady and keep the true poise. Many don't. They fail. They are swamped. The vision blurs. The judgment wavers. Action comes under the sway of blurred vision, and twisted judgment.

Emotion should never be allowed to take the reins and drive. When it is so, whatever the emotion be, grief or joy, love or hate, there's a runaway, a break-down and smash-up ahead. The will must always hold the lines hard and steady. It should be influenced fully by natural emotion, by knowledge, and by disciplined judgment. But the will must keep control.

Death, never lazy, has been running riot of late, with a ghoulish uncanny glee. The world's worst war has counted the dead into millions. Actual violence has been joined by strain, disease, and sheer want, in claiming occupants for the grave. The natural strain which death always puts on the living has been intensified terrifically.

An Aftermath of the War

And so it was quite the thing to be expected that there would be an intense revival of interest in the old questions about the dead, and especially about whether we can communicate with the dead. And it has come, with a rush.

The movement has swept these two English-speaking peoples like the wild-fire of the prairies that spreads and rages unchecked. Under various names, spiritualism, spiritism, psychic phenomena, occultism and so on, it is the old fire burning more intensely than ever, even in pulpits, as well as out of them.

There has suddenly sprung up unparalleled additions to the literature of the subject. In our own country decidedly more than a hundred new books have appeared since the Spring of 'Eighteen, with new titles being added every week. There are said to be nineteen periodicals devoted to spiritism as a cult, able to pay their own way. One book, from a British pen, is listed in the public libraries as among the five or six most in demand. One London society is said to have a collection of three thousand volumes dealing directly with various phases of spiritism.

And the mechanical means provided to facilitate so-called communication with the dead have been in common demand and use to such an extent as to be used to point witticisms in the daily papers.

The more recent name for this contrivance is very suggestive, a "ouija" board. The name is a mongrel combination of two languages, "oui," French; "ja," German; that is, "yes-yes." It will assent to anything you suggest, whatever your language, and give the comfortable feeling that you are right in your hopes and yearnings.

Communication with the Dead 127

Two prominent men in England have become leaders in the movement. One of these has made quite a remarkable visit to the United States. An able scientist in the physicist realm, with a noble presence, fine use of cultured language, and skilful publicity, he has had great crowds wherever he has gone.

It is interesting that in a recent review of the opinion of more than a hundred leading American scientists, educators and specialists in psychology, the concensus was decidedly against his stand and teaching, judged wholly from the scientific, scholarly standpoint. It has been suggested that if he had employed the same puerile methods in the physicist realm he would never have emerged from the shades of obscurity.

Yet one can be sympathetic with him to a certain degree, personally, while utterly opposed to his teaching. For as great an emotional nature as his, unsteadied by moorings, could easily be swept aside by the great personal grief that came to him through the war.

The other of these two is a gifted writer of detective stories, chiefly, which have been read wherever English is read. It is not surprising that these two Englishmen have had such a wide hearing among the unthinking.

Yet in neither case do the special training and achievement which have made these men so well and favorably known, give special qualification for sifting evidence, or of being competent judges, on this present subject. Rather it would take a specialized mental discipline to break away from their accustomed work, and acquire competence of judgment in examining a matter so utterly removed from their special studies.

But let us get to our question about communication with the dead. And it is most striking to note that this is one of the very oldest of questions. Its beginnings run far back into the mistiest past. This present wild-fire is not only not a new thing, but one of the oldest and grayest, its edges all frayed by the wear of time.

Communication with the dead, in some phase of it, is the main underpinning of nearly all the religions of the world, both civilized and savage. The two outstanding exceptions are Judaism and Christianity. Ancestor-worship, or the cult of the dead, is the staple of most religions from early Egyptian through Greek, Roman, Phoenician, up to present day Chinese and Japanese.

It is associated most in our thought today with China. With them the spirit of the dead father or other kinsman is supposed to enter the ancestral tablet and to commune with his living kin. He is supposed to do more, he favors and helps and protects his living kinsfolk. For a slavish fear really underlies their ancestor-worship, though perhaps unconsciously.

In its higher forms this ancestor-worship is an abnormal, morbid extension of proper veneration for one's parents and elders. It becomes an improper exaggeration of a perfectly proper thing. It easily degenerates into its lower form of communication with spirits, that is, into necromancy, witchcraft, and the like. Veneration degenerates into slavish fear and dread.

Three Groups

But now, let us face fairly the question: can we have communication with the dead? There are those who assert positively that we can. Their common teaching is that the spirits of the dead *do* come back to us, that they try to get into communication, and that the difficulty involved is because they and we are in two quite different spheres. And so, they say, there is naturally some difficulty, like in the use of two different languages until we have become learned in their use.

These people fall into three groups. At the lowest level are those who believe *in ghosts*. These are usually the ignorant and superstitious. Though it is surprising how common this sort of thing is among all classes. The ghosts are supposed to be spirits of human beings who have died, and who return to their former abodes. One strange feature of this belief is the terrible sense of fear that goes with it. It is as though loved ones had changed their character through death, and now would do harm.

I recall a sensible remark made by a simple man in a backward country district. A sense of terror had seized a certain group because the ghost of a recently deceased kinsman was thought to have come back. "Well," he said, "if he's in hell he can't come back; and if he's in heaven, he doesn't want to come back." But such sensible talk is not as common as one could wish.

Then **there are the** *professionals* who make a

livelihood by their art. These are commonly known today as mediums. That is the word in use now. They are supposed to supply the medium of communication between the two worlds. This is a very large class, to be found in all our cities on both sides of the water.

Sometimes they are called clairvoyants, which simply means those who can see clearly. The word is from the French, as is the other word commonly used, "seance," meaning simply a sitting or a session, used for the time spent in getting the alleged communication.

The third group is supposed to be on a higher level. These are the so-called *scientific investigators*. They profess to put the whole thing upon a scientific or scholarly basis. The common phrase here is psychical research. With this is associated the study of the character of hypnotism, mesmerism, magnetism, and the like.

And without any doubt there is here a wide legitimate sphere for research. Though one notes the constant tendency by some to drop to the lower levels. It is rather surprising what a degree of credulity can be shown in this research by some who are insistent on rigid evidence in other fields.

The British Society for Psychical Research has had on its rolls the names of many distinguished publicists and men prominent in various walks, though its activities seem controlled by a certain distinctive group with marked leanings toward the results they are eager to find. These are the three groups.

Communication with the Dead

An Uncharted Realm of Mental Science

It should be noted carefully here that there is a legitimate psychical research which belongs to the realm of mental science or psychology. There are certain functions of the mind that seem never to have been fully understood, nor adequately explained and defined.

Mental science, or psychology, as conventionally treated in all text books and schools, has ignored these functions. That's one extreme. The psychical specialists who attempt to treat the subject in a scholarly way do not as a rule, make clear analysis and distinctions. That's the other extreme. Without question there is here a field of research in mental science not yet adequately explored and charted.

There seem plainly to be mental traits or gifts or functions that properly belong to our natural stock of mental powers, but which seem to have been lost, or partially lost, through the hurt of sin. Some still have them in varying degree. But commonly we are so ignorant of just what they are that they seem uncanny to the common man.

These traits or functions are said to belong to the sub-conscious mind. That is they are working while we are unconscious of them. They are also said to belong to the subliminal mind. That is, the mind below the threshold of what we are conscious of. The thought is the same with both terms.

For instance one will have a premonition about a loved one who is at a distance, quite apart from any information that has come through the ordinary channels. He may have a similar premonition about some coming event. Without any doubt the Holy Spirit guides those in touch with him regarding such things. But distinctly in addition to this guidance, there is undoubtedly a mental trait that takes account of such things. But this is much more marked in some, and in others quite missing.

I have an intimate friend who has this sort of mental quality to rather a marked degree. For instance it comes to him that a certain one will call and will act in a certain detailed way. And so it turns out.

He has had the experience of driving along a country road and of seeing places and people and incidental happenings as though in his mind's eye, and only so. Then after driving maybe two or three miles he would come across exactly what his spirit vision had discerned.

He is an earnest Christian man, somewhat familiar with the dangers we are speaking of here. And he follows the settled principle of not seeking to tamper with a realm unfamiliar, but instead prayerfully to hold all his powers subject to the Holy Spirit's constant guidance.

One remarkable thing he constantly experiences is the strong impulse to pray for certain ones, indeed an intense drawing aside for such prayer, as though the one brought to mind were in peculiar need or danger or temptation. And repeatedly the knowledge has come afterwards of the sore need or danger or special temptation, and the deliverance.

If one find himself possessed of some such gift in some marked degree, he should pray quietly over it. Dedicate it, with *all* your powers, to the Master. Never seek to use it save as you use any better-understood power, by the Holy Spirit's gracious guidance, in practical ways. Be cautious, just because of the element of not clearly understanding the gift.

Something akin to this sort of thing, though quite distinct, is the experience of some saintly people, as they near death's door. As they draw near the veil between this and the spirit world, seems to grow thinner. As the physical powers weaken, the spirit vision seems able to see what could not be seen before.

As Stephen stood in the midst of the raging murderous mob bent on his blood, the eyes of his spirit were opened. He saw what was clearly beyond the range of physical eyesight. And what did he see? Jesus! glorified, standing at the Father's right hand.[1]

I recall as though yesterday the light that came into the face of a dear saint as she was slipping out over into the King's presence. She looked quietly intently up, as though she could see some one or some thing which we could not see.

A delighted look lightened her eyes and face. Then she looked around at those surrounding her bed, as though she would say "Can't you see, too?" Then she sank into the sleep that

[1] Acts vii. 55.

carried her spirit into the presence of Him she loved so devotedly.

The word telepathy has been coined for something akin to this, though distinctly different. That is the communication of one person with another in close sympathy without the ordinary recognized means of communication. One mind seems to communicate with another without words, looks, gestures, or the like. Some are much more sensitive to this sort of thing than others.

Without any doubt our common ignorance of these little-understood mental traits or powers, has been skilfully made use of by professional experts who themselves are peculiarly sensitive in these directions, and have carefully cultivated that sensitiveness. There is apt to be with these professional spiritists a subtle blend of what is quite legitimate with that which is distinctly illegitimate, and is cunning trickery. And the uninformed man, perhaps under the stress of some great grief, is quite swept off his feet.

The Responses That Do Come

Now these are the people, these three groups, who answer yes to our question. They say there *is* a response to this attempt to communicate. And let it be said here quite plainly and positively that *there are responses.* There can be no question of that.

But please note keenly, *the character of these responses.* Without exception they are vague, indefinite, insufficient, frequently childish. They are double-meaninged; that is they can be turned this way, or this other opposite way. They sometimes are dovetailed with exquisite shrewdness into suggestions given or drawn out.

If indeed these responses were communications from our loved dead it would be rather disheartening. For judging from these, it would seem clear that those we loved have undergone a decided decadence in their mental powers. The commonsense with which they used to talk seems painfully missing.

Now, the intense, vital question is *where do these undoubted responses come from?* The spiritists or mediums say they come from the spirits of our dead talking with us. Certain psychologists, who specialize on the psychical side of things, say they come from within ourselves, from the workings of our sub-conscious minds.

After long careful, prayerful study I have reached the deliberate conclusion that there are *five possible sources* from which they may come, and only these five. These experts say they do come from our loved dead.

They may come from a subtle interplay of the inner working of two human minds, the mind of the enquirer and that of the professional. That would make it wholly mental. They may come through the cunning deception of the expert working on an overwrought emotional condition of the enquirer, or, dealing with undisciplined, untaught, credulous enquirers or observers.

They may come, are you listening quietly, for this is tremendous, yet I am saying it very deliberately, they may come from demons. **Or,** they may come through a subtle mixture of two or more of these, inextricably interwoven. I am quite clear that all these five things must be taken into account, and that they cover all the ground.

Our English friend, who lectured so widely in the United States, in response to the criticism that these responses are so unsatisfactory and childish, is reported to have replied in effect that *the fact of a response* established that there is communication with the one desired. It seems quite incredible that a man of his intelligence could have made such a reply. It is so utterly childish in its ignorance of the various possible sources of such phenomena.

Now, let me go one step further. I have come to a clear settled personal conviction about where these responses come from. This conviction has come slowly. It has come, not through ignoring any evidence, but weighing everything most carefully.

I have carefully read ghost stories and allied literature. I have talked, both here and in Great Britain and Continental Europe, with sensible people, who have had unusual experiences. I have tried to examine the Psychical Research Society, and similar, literature. And though I have never gone to a spiritistic seance, as a matter of principle and of deep conviction, yet I have talked with those who have.

And I have come to three deliberate conclusions. First, human spirits do *not* return to talk with us. There is never communication with them. Second, haunted houses, apparitions, and the like, can always be explained fully, either by the presence of demons, or by the working of our subtler mental processes, that is, by subjective impressions, hallucinations, and the like.

And third, the responses that come through spiritistic experts, are never messages from the dead. Some of them are from demons. And their purpose in this we shall see in a few moments. Some are the unconscious interplay of the subtler mental processes of the two in touch, the enquirer and the expert. And some are simply *deliberate skilful deception* by the spiritistic expert.

It is of intense interest to note the conditions which these experts say are essential to getting what they call good results, namely, there must be a non-critical spirit. That really means with them a non-scrutinizing spirit. There should instead be a passive, acquiescent, sympathetic spirit. The more fully one can yield up all self-control over his faculties, and yield wholly to the influences of the expert, the better the results gotten, they say.

The Authoritative Answer

But we haven't really got our answer yet. The authoritative answer is yet to come. And it *is* authoritative. It leaves nothing to be said. When we get that the case is settled. It is the answer of this old Book of God. It becomes of intense interest to note that this Book recognizes this question, discusses it fully, and answers it flatly and fully and positively.

138 Quiet Talks on Life After Death

Let us look at this authoritative answer.

The Bible is an index to the moral customs and conditions of the nations surrounding the old Jewish nation. And that means practically of all the nations of that old world. For the Jewish domain lay at the center. All the nations touched that domain directly or indirectly.

Every national culture influenced its life, as in the after centuries every civilization marched its armies over that territory. The prohibitions contained in the Ten Commandments, with the numerous detailed prohibitions grouped with them, became a perfect bit of mirror reflecting common moral conditions among these surrounding nations.

From the earliest times there was in all these nations a class of experts in the cult of the dead, the foretelling of the future, the settling of doubtful questions, interpretation of dreams, and in general the magical and mysterious. Practically this was the priestly class. For this sort of thing was connected with, and made up a large part of, their religion.[1] Such a class of professionals flourished at various times among the Jews though expressly prohibited.[2]

The various names by which these magical experts were known are significant. They let in a flood of light as to these forbidden practices. There's an index given in Moses' farewell talks in the Plains of Moab.[3]

[1] Genesis xli. 8; Exodus vii. 11, 22; viii. 7; Daniel ii. 2, 10, 27; iv. 6, 7.
[2] Samuel xv. 23; xxviii. 3, 8-15. 2 Kings xxi. 6; xxiii. 24.
[3] Deuteronomy xviii. 9-14.

Communication with the Dead 139

"There shall not be found with thee any one that maketh his son or daughter to *pass through the fire,* one that *useth divination,* one that practices *augury,* or an *enchanter,* or a *sorcerer,* or a *charmer,* or a *consulter with a familiar spirit,* or a *wizard,* or a *necromancer.*"

These are grouped together as one class, equally abominable to God, with nine varying names according to methods used, or the pretensions made. Then the whole class is grouped up under two names, augury and diviners. One of these names deals distinctively with consulting the dead, that is, necromancer, one who consults the dead, and divines or foretells by that means.

The name used for another one of these lets in a flood of clear light on the whole class, that is, "a consulter with a *familiar spirit.*" Familiar spirit is the old English word for devil or demon. The word underneath here is one of those used for a devil or demon.

That is to say, the pretended purpose of all these was communication with the dead. The *real* purpose underneath was communication with demons or evil spirits. In other words, all this was *devilcraft.* So the Holy Spirit reveals plainly here. Other names are sometimes used for the same general craft, astrologers, stargazers, monthly prognosticators, sooth-sayers.[1]

It is of interest to note that the designation, "black art," and "black magic," which are commonly used for devilcraft grow out of the word necromancer. By an accidental slip of a single

[1] Isaiah xlvii. 12, 13; Jeremiah xxvii. 9, 10.

letter, "c" was changed to "g," and so the word read, negromancer, that is negro, a black man, negromancer, one who divined by black, or dark, or forbidden means. That term "black art" has come to be quite commonly used for all devilcraft. It is synonymous with sorcery and witchcraft.

Now the thing that stands out with unmistakeable emphasis is this: all this sort of thing was forbidden by God. It was forbidden in the strongest language. It was characterized as the very worst sort of wickedness. And it was to be met with the extremest penalty. Note some of the passages. One in particular stands out as a sort of index to all. It is spoken to Israel at a time when the nation was far down the spiritual decline that at least disrupted it.

"And when they shall say unto you, seek unto them that have familiar spirits (demons) and unto the wizards that chirp, and that mutter:— should not a people seek unto their *God? Should they seek unto the dead on behalf of the living?* To the teaching and testimony (of God's word)! If they speak not according to this word, surely there is no morning (that is, no dawning, no hope) for them."[1]

Pretty plain talk that. How peculiarly it fits in with common life today! These devil craftsmen were aggressively at work. But it was a time of sore stress in the nation. There was sore need of guidance. What would they do? How wholesomely simple the answer. Go to God's Book. It has plain teaching. It will tell

[1] Isaiah viii. 19-20.

you; and more, if you don't, things will go bad, only bad, with you, sooner or later.

Listen to these three passages spoken, be it keenly marked, by *God Himself,* and simply recited by Moses with the great Ten Commandments:—"Thou shalt not suffer a sorceress to live."[1] "Ye shall not use enchantments, nor practice augury." "Turn ye not unto them that have familiar spirits (demons), nor unto the wizards; seek them not out, to be defiled by them. I am Jehovah your God."[2]

"The soul that turneth unto them that have familiar spirits (demons), and unto the wizards, to play the harlot after them, I will even set my face against that soul, and will cut him off from among his people."

"A man or a woman that hath a familiar spirit (demon) or that is a wizard, shall surely be put to death; they shall be stoned with stones."[3]

Could stronger language be used? These practices were defiling, befouling, morally dirty. They were classed with the worst sort of sexual impurity. They were the worst sort of enmity to God. They were to be visited with the extreme penalty, death, and death in one of its most painful drastic forms, stoning.

Another of these stinging characterizations comes from the lips of Samuel. He is talking with King Saul. And if any body in this old Book could use plain tense stinging talk it was

[1] Exodus xxii. 18.
[2] Leviticus xix. 26, 31.
[3] Leviticus xx. 6, 27.

Samuel. Listen to him, and watch Saul's face whitening under the writhing rebuke.

"Rebellion (that is, simply failure to obey God) is as witchcraft (devil craft), and stubbornness (being set in your own way even against God's way) is extreme iniquity and devil-worship."[1] In other words, these evil, occult, magical, practices were the extreme form of badness. They were devilish. That's the superlative degree.

It is striking to note that these things become the common touchstone of the worst wickedness. National reformations hit directly at them.[2] Bad kings, revived them.[3] It was because of such practices, and others kin to them, that the Canaanitish nations had been cast out, and that long after, Israel went to pieces.[4] They are repeatedy referred to in the denunciation of the prophets.[5]

With these sharp-cut words from the Old Testament in mind it becomes of intense interest to turn to the other end of the Book. Paul in his old age, with spirit vision made sensitive by the Holy Spirit's touch, discerns that in the end of the Church period,

"Some (in the Church) shall fall away from the (true) faith, giving heed to seducing (that is misleading, "vagabond") demons, and to things taught by demons through pretended good

---

[1] 1 Samuel xv. 23 partly paraphrased.
[2] 1 Samuel xxviii. 3, 9; 2 Kings xxiii. 24 et al.
[3] 2 Kings xxi. 6; 2 Chronicles xxxiii. 6.
[4] 2 Kings xvi. 3; xvii. 7.
[5] Isaiah xix. 3; xxix. 4; xliv. 25; Jeremiah xxvii. 9, 10; Micah iii. 6. 7, 11; Malachi iii. 5.

Communication with the Dead

men who really speak lies, and whose consciences are seared as with a hot iron."[1]

The Evil Purpose Underneath

Here then is the plain teaching of God's Word. Nothing could be plainer nor more explicit. Attempted communication with the dead is allied directly with the worst black art. It is grouped with devilcraft. It is really dealing with demons.

It is a distinctly forbidden realm, marked sharply off. The prohibition could not be more explicit and express. The prohibition is put in strongest language. Such practices are characterized as defiling, befouling, abominable. They were to be visited with the extreme penalty.

But, there's even more than this to be most carefully noted. That is the *utter incompetence* of such attempts to give what we desire. There simply is not, and cannot be, any such communication with our loved ones who have gone. So that pretensions of this sort are a deliberate deception.

The fact that there are such pretensions, made so positively and aggressively, at once becomes significant. There is clearly a purpose back of this. It is a purpose of evil. Indeed it is a purpose of the Evil One himself. He is clearly the one behind all this sort of thing.

And *his purpose* is as plain as it is brazen and startling. *He wants to get control of men.* He can get control only through their consent, ex-

---

[1] 1 Timothy iv. 1-2 paraphrased.

tracted under deception when not openly given. Demoniacs are extreme instances of such control. They are human beings possessed and controlled to such an extent as to have lost self-control *completely.*

They really are too much under demon control to be serviceable to the devil. It's a case where the demons are not kept in hand by their chief. They get out of *his* control. Demoniacs in the Gospel are instances of this sort of thing. They can be found in heathen lands today, though their families are commonly ashamed to have the fact known.

In the western world the uncontrollable cases of demon possession are mostly in the insane asylum. But these likewise are too far gone to be serviceable to the Evil One. He prefers simply enough control of a man so he can have use of him in the usual avenues of life, mingling among his fellows.

The danger of tampering with this sort of thing is terribly real. I remember a small book that came into my hands years ago in London. It was devoted to the discussion of the serious dangers attending practices of this sort. It was not written at all from a Christian standpoint; indeed just the opposite.

That makes its warnings more pointed. The writer was not concerned apparently with the question of right or wrong, but only with the danger to one's mental powers and self-control. In speaking of those who attempt communication with the spirit world, he said, quoting freely, *"They open a door that by and by they cannot shut, when they earnestly want to shut it."* And he went on to instance cases he knew of the deplorable disastrous results that had followed, including his own experiences. Even our well-known English author and lecturer, already referred to, warns his readers against the dangers attending spiritistic experiments. This is very significant.

I recall a man I came in touch with in Northern Germany some years ago. He was an honest, earnest, simple-hearted peasant. He had been eager for certain experiences that others of his acquaintance had. He was plainly demon-possessed, and yet against his will. The evidence was unmistakeable to me. Happily through prayer and instruction he was set free.

But I was struck at the time with the unusually clear statement he made to me of how his trouble came. He said, "I was ignorant of the danger; I opened the door; the evil spirit came in; and I couldn't free myself of his presence." These illustrate the terrible dangers of tampering with such things.

The Witch of Endor

But now before leaving this part of our talk where the Scripture is being quoted, I want to refer to two passages more. These come at the first flush as a distinct surprise. There are two instances in the Bible of communication with those who have died. They stand out sharply as the only two. They were plainly planned by God himself. And they stand out in such detailed contrast as must be painful in the extreme to those believing in the devil's sort of communications.

The first of these is the case of Samuel and the witch of Endor.[1] Look at it briefly. King Saul, who sought the witch's help, was *out of touch with God.* That is an outstanding feature of the story. Twice he had openly disobeyed God's explicit command. And he was the national leader. That made a bad thing so much worse. Whatever he did, the crowds would do.[2]

Now in an emergency (it's always an emergency that tempts one so sorely), he sought an illegitimate means of guidance. He himself had forbidden witchcraft under penalty of death. Now, disguised, he makes a secret night journey up north to Endor to consult a witch there. He succeeds in overcoming her cautious regard for her own safety in doing a prohibited thing, and asks her to bring Samuel up for consultation. Samuel had been dead some little time.

Now the striking thing to note is, that Samuel did come and talk with Saul. But it is quite clear that *the witch had nothing to do with Samuel's coming.* Instead she was utterly taken back, astonished and startled beyond measure by what happened. The whole thing was taken quite out of her hands.

To her intense fright a spirit actually came up before her eyes. There is instant identification of who it is. It is Samuel. No one was better

[1] 1 Samuel xxviii. 3-19.
[2] 1 Samuel xiii. 8-14; xv. 1-23.

known to the common people, for years the nation's great leader. Her recognition of him is immediate and unquestioning.

At once a startled cry comes from her lips. The common translation in the King James' version and in the Revisions is, "she cried with a loud voice." A more full accurate translation would be *"she was greatly startled and gave out suddenly a piercing shriek of distress."*

Her shrewd native cunning made her quick to sense instantly that this disguised man consulting her was the King himself. Samuel, who had put Saul on the throne, actually coming up in person in this unprecedented way, naturally suggested to her keen wits that this other was Saul. For the break between Samuel and Saul had been open talk.

This is the first thing to note. The witch had nothing to do with Samuel's coming. This was a new experience to her, and a distinctly unwelcome experience. Something was happening wholly out of her realm of incantation.

A second thing to notice is the contrast of the sharpest kind between this communication from Samuel and *all* so-called communications from the dead. The latter are characteristically vague, cryptic, or cunningly double-meaninged and distinctly below the known intelligence of the one supposed to be speaking. And further they seek to leave an agreeable impression.

But, here, Samuel speaks in his accustomed way. He gave definite detailed information, of a very unwelcome sort about the triple tragic happenings of the morrow. Saul would be defeated by the Philistines. He would lose the kingdom, and he would meet death, and his sons with him. And with this was a stinging rebuke that must have had a decidedly unpleasant familiarity to Saul as it cut its edge into the quick.

And now, mark keenly the influence of this incident on these impressionable Hebrew Orientals. The thing was commonly known. It could not be hid. The grapevine telegraph took it to every corner of Israel. It was the talk of the nation. *And,* more, it plainly gave a sharp set-back to witchery and all like practices.

There is no mention or allusion to such things for at least half a century, though they had been prevalent up to this time. An awe or fear comes over the people. They are afraid to attempt this sort of thing. God had rebuked it. This is the only thing of the sort in the whole Old Testament.

The other exceptional instance is the appearance of Moses on the Mount of Transfiguration.[1] This is referred to only because it plainly is an instance of communication with the dead. But it is recognized at once that it belongs to a wholly different realm from that being discussed, and as much above it as the heavens are above the earth.

Moses had died sixteen centuries before. Now he plainly appears. He appears in company with Elijah, the fiery denouncer of all witchery and devilcraft. His identity is undoubted. Recognition of him is immediate. He talks with our Lord Jesus. He talks too, on a subject pecu-

[1] Matthew xvii. 1-8 and parallels.

liarly obnoxious to the devil and to the whole tribe of the black art under whatever guise, namely, the sacrificial death of Jesus on the cross.

These are the two exceptions in this Book. And plainly they do but put into a sharper prominence the terrible characterizations and prohibitions of this Book on the whole brood of practices of devilcraft and its allied arts. Plainly in these two instances God deemed it wise for some practical purpose to have these occurrences take place and be recorded. And in both cases *He* took the *initiative*.

Meeting Our Human Need

The question of praying for the dead is an intensely interesting one. It is on the other side of this subject; not seeking help *from* the dead, but seeking to be helpful to them. The custom of praying for the dead has been in the Church, to varying extent, since the second century. It is common in certain sections of the Church of England today, and in certain communions that recognize that Church's leadership.

There is only one passage of Scripture quoted in its support, namely II Timothy 1:18. But this is quoted on the supposition that one, Onesiphorus, was dead, which is quite possible but not at all certain. The utter silence of Scripture on the subject, apart from this doubtful passage, would seem distinctly significant.

We are not told to pray for the dead. If our loved ones are in our Lord's presence prayer seems needless. If they are not, are they past the influence of prayer? The last chapter touches on this. Meanwhile praise can well take the place of prayer as the names of our dear ones come to our lips at prayer time.

Now there remains just one word more to add. And it is a word of deepest significance. Grief is still epidemic. Hearts are still sore and bleeding. The hearthstone is still lonely. Every meal time brings up heartbreaking memories. Loneliness still eats its acid way in.

We're hungrier than ever for fellowship. We're so needing plain straight guidance in our every day affairs. We do want to know about our loved ones. Is there no close-up, warm, help for us these days when grief drips its ceaseless rain all the day and far into the night?

Well, there's an answer to these human heart cries. And it is immediate and plain and full, and has a real human heart throb in it. There's a Friend who will share your lonely corner with you, and fill it and you with warmth and fellowship and glad song.

He's real, this Friend. He has the human touch. He knows all about things down here. He knows what it is to lose a dear friend through unexpected death. There isn't one experience down here that He doesn't know by the feel, except experiences that come through wrong choice.

And so He *can* tell you what to do in emergencies and tight corners and everywhere else. And He *will* do it. And more than that He is in as close touch with your loved one who's gone as with you. He is your connecting link.

What do I mean? Whom am I talking about. Listen, while I try to get past the sometimes hardened shell of familiar words to the tense throbbing realities inside them. He's the Holy Spirit. He understands by the feel, all that Jesus went through.

But there is more. He is the Spirit of the glorified enthroned Jesus. He knows all our true human feelings *and* He knows all the divine power. For He is truly God, as well as human. His coming to live in you is so real a thing that it couldn't be more real. He spoke in this Book of God. He *speaks* in it. He will talk through its pages to you to-day. He will talk directly to your inmost spirit. He will surround you with the atmosphere of His own presence.

Getting in Touch

But, you say, just *how* can He become real to me like you say. Listen, the answer is so simple, yet it is radical. It is this: surrender yourself to the Lord Jesus as *Master* as well as Saviour. Make that surrender a habitual thing.

In a sane wholesome way make *this* the touchstone of your daily life—*to please Him.* Put His Word in the central place, the first place, before all other reading. Get a bit of *quiet time* alone with it, daily. Drink it in. Devour its contents. Breathe in its spirit. Absorb it. Brood over it.

Learn to spend the day with God. He *is* with you, and in you, in the person of His Holy Spirit. Thank Him for His presence. Do it daily. Sing

Him a song of praise. Do it habitually. Talk to Him when you don't need to ask for something. Practice His presence. He is there by your side as you are reading this. Learn to spend the day with Him. All this sort of thing will discipline your judgment.

You will become keen to know the meaning of "watch and pray". Watch is for the subtle crafty enemy, masquerading much these days in his "angel of light" costume, with unctuous voice, and reverent mien. You learn to pray with one eye open. The two must be balanced in your practice, with wholesome sanity, trained vision, and disciplined judgment.

But somebody says that this doesn't help you a bit, for you are not in touch with God. Your mind is tormented with doubts about God, and His Word, and all this. Well, here's a bit for you *if you're honest*. That may be a big *if*. But honesty is the first essential.

Listen. My honestly skeptical friend *can get a response direct from God to his own soul,* if he really wants it. There's a pierced Hand on the knob at your door right now. There's someone waiting, waiting now on your door step, waiting to come in. And He will give you a *response* that will *satisfy* your deepest longings.

A mother with troubled face, spoke to John Bartholomew Gough at the close of one of his famous temperance lectures. She had a darling boy, a man, but her boy. He called himself a skeptic. And the mother's heart was like to break. Would Mr. Gough talk with her boy. That was her request.

They met. The young man poured out his doubts. He seemed really sincere. Mr. Gough listened in his friendly way. Finally he said, "Why don't you pray? Prayer is a natural thing." But whom should he pray to? He didn't think there was a God. Mr. Gough said, "Why not pray to Love. You believe in love. You believe in your dear mother's love for you. That's a pure holy passion." That touched a sensitive spot. The young man said he would.

In his bedroom that night he knelt with closed eyes, and cried out passionately, "Oh, Love!" Instantly, though so softly, the words seemed spoken in his inner being, "God is Love." And at once, he followed the impulse that came, and cried out, "Oh, God." Again so softly, the words he knew by heart, seemed spoken within, "God so loved the world that He gave His Only Begotten."

And again, yielding to the quick impulse in his spirit, his lips cried out, "Oh, Christ." And at once something came. An exquisite sense of peace stole into his spirit, as he was kneeling. The *fog of doubts,* where were they? A thousand questions remained unanswered, but there was that singular quiet sense of peace within. He was *in touch* with Him, who made peace by the blood of the Cross.

Any body who will, can get in touch. For He, the Man who was done to death for us, is now within reach. The honest heart reaching can get in touch. And that touch *with Him,* answers all questions and needs.

V

WHAT IS DEATH?

Pleasing, But Not True

Death means death of the body. That is the common meaning, the plain everyday meaning. That is the biggest thing we're conscious of. It's the thing we feel most.

The body we loved so much lies lifeless. It is laid away under the sod. We do not see it. There is the utter absence of the loved one. The spirit that looked out of the bodily eyes has gone from us. The break between body and spirit is complete. He is dead. The separation between him and us is entire.

That is the commonest meaning. And that meaning is quite correct so far as it goes. But it is a limited meaning. It's the thing that absorbs us most, if not to the exclusion of everything else. Yet there is more. And we want to talk in a purely practical way about that more.

There is a common teaching about death that is directly opposite to the Biblical teaching. It belittles death to the point of practically ignoring it. Though of course, the fact of bodily death cannot be ignored.

Death is pictured as a mere transition. It is a natural step from one state of existence to another, it is said. It is not an enemy, and not a thing to be dreaded. This teaching is marked by vague looseness of statement. Clean-cut thinking, sharp distinctions, clear careful definitions are absent.

In their place is a mixture of partial truths expressed in beautiful language, with the clear-cut, sharp lines of truth blurred. Some choice bits of literature have been produced. They have found their way freely into Christian circles.

Death is likened to certain changes of development that take place in the natural order. The caterpillar passes into the chrysalis form, and by and by emerges a rarely beautiful butterfly. And death among men is likened to these transitions.

The whole thing of death is made to appear as simple and natural a transition as these. This sounds very beautiful. And it is acceptable to many folks, if not most. They like it. But it entirely ignores certain *facts*. It is quite opposed to the plain teaching of the Book of God. And the practical effect is not only not good. It is bad.

It tends to blur the fact that the time of death is a time of moral adjustment. And these adjustments hinge on our choices and on our character. It belittles or ignores what Jesus did for us when He died. It tends to keep us from putting choice of Christ as Saviour in the big place, where it belongs, in our thinking. And it lulls us into a sort of fool's paradise that everything is all right with us regardless of how we've lived, or what we've believed.

The Meaning Pictured

Now, I want to turn to the Old Book. It is very striking to find in its very opening pages a definition of death. For that is what it practically is.

It is a pictured definition. And that makes it easy for us all to get. For all the world loves and looks at a picture. And when some skilled artist who's studied it, points out the colorings, the lights and shades, and groupings and postures, it becomes fascinating.

Look at this picture. It's in a garden. Man's friendly God is walking through the garden, side by side with the man. They are fellows together in their fine friendliness of feeling. Man's Fellow is showing him about the garden, making him familiar with his new home. They stop under a tree.

And there the word is quietly and clearly spoken: *"In the day thou eatest thereof thou shalt surely die."*[1] It's the tree of choice. It's the practical touchstone of their continued sweet companionship together. God is pleading for the man to use his power of choice *right*. Their fine fellowship together was the plea, a tremendous plea. God was saying, as father to son, "Let us always keep in fullest touch."

But it was a matter for the man's decision. By using his power of choice in choosing right, constantly, he would become like God in character as well as in sovereignty of choice. That's the first time death is referred to. The actual phrase used is this, "dying, thou shalt die." There is a beginning, a process, and a finished result.

Then comes the temptation story, the yielding

[1] Genesis ii. 17.

to temptation, and the break of fellowship. Now, note keenly, what "die" actually meant to these two early kinsfolk of ours. They ate the forbidden fruit. At once they were conscious of some difference in themselves. There came a self-consciousness regarding their bodies which was not there before. It seems not good, for they do something to remove or correct it.

There was no actual change in them from what had been before, *except* mental or in spirit. The forbidden act made a change. They were separated from what they had been before. It proves to be a separation in spirit from God. Things are not between them as they had been.

Then comes a second step. They try to hide from God. Already they misunderstand Him. They think because they cannot see Him that he cannot see them. The ostrich had an early imitator. But they want to get away from God. That's the big thing.

The separation between Him and them is increasing, and it is increasing by their action. There's no difference in God. But plainly there's a longing for separation from Him. And that means there *is* a separation *in spirit,* grown wider by the longing to get away from His presence.

Then comes the third stage in the process. They are driven out of the immediate conscious presence of God. Though, as noted elsewhere, the driving out was almost certainly a moral thing, their sense of the presence of God now influencing them to leave that presence voluntarily.

Then comes the story of the awful break in the

home. That inner spirit, that sought separation from God among the trees of the garden, grows strong and passionate in the home. It leads Cain to seek a forced separation from one whose presence he has come to hate.

Then comes the final stage in this pictured meaning of "die" or death. Nine hundred and some odd years later it is said of Adam "and he died." God had said, *"in the day* thou eatest thereof dying thou shalt die". The dying began on that day. Yet bodily death was deferred for over nine hundred years.

No Change in God

Plainly enough death here means separation in spirit from God. It has a beginning. It continues as a process, intensifying in character. It is a final result. It affects the man's spirit toward God at once. It comes, by and by, to affect his body.

The hold of the human spirit on the body in which it lives is affected. Bodily conditions are affected. And that grows and intensifies until the spirit and body can no longer hold together. The separation of spirit from God comes to include bodily conditions.

It is noticed further that there is in this picture no change of action or attitude on God's part. The separation is a grief to Him. He continues His creative sustaining touch just as **far** as he is allowed to. The separation is wholly on man's part. It is in his spirit. It is in his *will*. He *wants* to get away. That finally results in the full separation that eventually brings bodily death.

Let it be noted very keenly that here death is an unnatural thing. It is a break in the natural order. It clearly enough was not in the original plan. It couldn't be. It is a direct result of break of touch with God. God never planned separation of any sort from man. And, at the core, that's just what death is. Life is full contact with God. Death is the reverse, a break in that contact. Plainly if the wire's cut the current can't get through.

It will be noticed that in this pictured definition there are two stages to death. There is the present or immediate. This is in one's spirit, or inner attitude toward God. There comes a change there at once when the break with God occurs. And God calls it death.

Then there is the second stage, the death to the body. That did not come till long afterwards. It is really a less thing than the other. Though it is the big thing in our common thought of death. The deeper, more serious thing, was in the inner spirit. That happened at once, and went on increasing in its grip and influence.

Here then is the pictured definition of what death means. It is the reverse of life. Life is full touch of spirit or heart with God. Any break in that touch means the loss of life, in some measure, and that is called death. This death is a thing of growth.

It moves from one stage to a deeper. It eventually comes to include death of the body. That is the big thing in our common thinking, but not in this Book. Now, this gives the meaning of death throughout this old Book of God. Put in so distinctly at the very beginning it clearly set the standard of meaning throughout.

Tracing the Trail

Now take a thoughtful run through the Book. Do it for yourself. Plainly it is a sheer impossibility to quote the long string of passages. But we can follow the trail of the definition. It is an easy trail to follow. And when one has followed it to the end, another run through brings to one's attention the countless illustrations. The separation of spirit which the definition emphasizes as the crucial thing colors the narrative from end to end.

Now, just a few looks at that trail. Death is separation in one's spirit from God. It affects one's spirit at once, and with a growing intensity. It affects one's body at once, imperceptibly, increasing gradually until it quite loses contact with the human spirit inhabiting it, within certain time limits.[1]

Death is the immediate logical outcome of sin. It is not a result of arbitrary action on God's part. Sin is death in the green; death is sin dead ripe. Sin is death begun; death is sin in its final finished shape. Here is the grammar of the verb to sin. Present tense, to sin; first future tense, to suffer; second future tense, death. The verb becomes a noun; the pliable verb a hardened, set noun.[2]

---

[1] Matthew viii. 22; Luke xv. 24, 32; Romans viii. 6; Ephesians ii. 1, 5; v. 14; 1 Timothy v. 6; Revelation iii. 1.
[2] Romans v. 12; vi. 21, 23.

What is Death? 161

Death does not mean merely bodily death,[1] though, of course, it comes to include that. It is not cessation of existence. Spirit never ceases to be. It cannot. The rich man still lived, quite possibly against his will, after his body was dead.[2] And death is as clearly not being asleep. For spirit never sleeps. The same reference covers that.

Death is not a natural thing. It is unnatural. It is a break in the natural order, and so, being a break, it is a thing painful in itself. It is natural to dread death, and to shrink from it. Death is an enemy, intruding upon a forbidden domain. That word "enemy" sums up the whole case here.[3]

Death, from its beginning to its end, passes through three stages. The first stage is the break of spirit with God. It is the rupture of friendship or fellowship with Him. Man was made to be God's fellow. And his remaining in that relation depends on his own desire, his choice and action.[4]

God eagerly longs for that fellowship, but only on the level where fellowship belongs, that is, when it is freely given. That's the first stage. It begins at once with the beginning of wrong choice. This is the worst, the most damnable stage, thus far. It is spirit death. It goes to the very roots.

[1] 1 Timothy v. 6; Revelation iii. 1; Ephesians ii. 1, 5; v. 4.
[2] Luke xvi. 19-31.
[3] 1 Corinthians xv. 16.
[4] Genesis ii. 17, with most of the quotations already made.

It puts the dry rot of death into the very seed of life. It is death by suicide. The man cuts himself off from the source of his life. It means separation from God, separation of spirit, of heart. This reveals the bigness of what Christ must do when He's allowed to. He has to make a wholly new start.[1]

The second stage is the thing that bulks so big with us when we speak of death, that is, death of the body. The break between the human spirit and its body becomes complete. That break of spirit with God, working imperceptibly from the moment of the break, now affects the body in the extreme degree.

This is the least part of death. It is the temporary stage. And this stage is for all, believers and others alike, up to the limit of time when Christ comes again. Then there comes a change for those in touch with Him.

There is the third stage. This is the final, the permanent stage. This is not for all. It is only for those who incorrigibly insist in their choice of leaving God and Christ out. It is called "the second death." The first death is that spirit death already mentioned. This is that same first death in its final hardened form.[2]

Five Things Jesus Did

This brings us up sharply to just what Jesus did. It makes us see what a desperate task He undertook. It was nothing less than dealing with

[1] John iii. 3-6.
[2] Revelation ii. 11; xx. 6, 14; xxi. 8.

dead men. And the only way of doing it was to begin a new life within. In the beginning it was simply a matter of creation. But now, of a new creation, with the wreck of the old one to handle and clear away.

Man was enslaved to Satan.[1] That slavery must be broken. But death was the stamp of the slavery, Satan's mark of control. Death must then be put to death, and he that had the power of death must be throttled.

Sin itself, with all the long damnable heart-breaking human story that has worked out of that break with God, became a slander on God's character and on God's management of the world. For God had let things run on in their bad way, instead of clearing the whole thing up at once, as He could rightly have done.

Then, too, it must be made clear what sort of a God God is, and why He has let things run on without prompt settlement. And then our hearts had become hardened against God. That separation brought hardening. And the hardening grew steadily harder, and yet more obstinately hard. That spirit death had penetrated clear into the inner marrow of our hearts.

Now, hush your hearts, and look with bated breath and reverently bowed heads at what Jesus did. He got into touch with us men, first of all. He lived, simply lived, a simple true human life, in all its commonplace round of duty and temptation, for thirty years, ten-elevenths of his full span of life. So He got in touch with us. So

[1] Romans vi. 16.

He really was one of us. So He kept in fullest touch with the Father in the daily round of a common human life.

Then He voluntarily gave His life up and out for us. He took upon Himself the death that belonged to us, death of body, aye, far more, and deeper, and bitterer, the death of spirit that was bound up with separation from the Father's conscious presence. That's the meaning of that heart-breaking cry, "Why didst thou forsake me?" He took upon Himself *all* that was coming to us.

He went down into the jaws of death, into the belly of hell. And there He put Death to death. He throttled it past any reviving. Through going to death himself, he utterly annihilated the power of him that has the power of death, that is the devil himself.[1] Than having effectively dealt that death blow, He quietly rose up again, out of death's domain, back toward the true center of gravity of His own life.

And when He came up He brought something up with Him, a great priceless something. He brought up life, His own life, a new sort of deathless life that could never know any taint of death. He brought it up into plain view where all might see, and so could make their new choice, the choice of Himself, as Saviour and Redeemer and Master.[2]

So He settled up our sin score, set us free of our slavery to sin, gave us a new eternal sort of

[1] Hebrews ii. 14.
[2] 2 Timothy i. 10 paraphrased.

life, vindicated God's patient enduring of sin's havoc, and broke our hearts with His untellable love.

And, now, anybody who'll get in touch of heart with Him, Christ, will escape death and have life. He will pass out of that separation which is death into the full touch that is life.[1] Yet freedom from the smaller item of death, bodily death, is not promised. In its place is promised a rising up out of the grave for our bodies even as His rose.[2] And then something more and greater yet is promised. That is, such victory in our spirits over the dark fearsome enemy, death, that when it does come to our bodies we shall greet it with a joyous shout of victory.[3] And meanwhile there remains always with us the glad possibility that His own return to earth shall spare us that last touch with our old enemy.

But Jesus does yet more. He's not through with death yet. Twice over we are told that he has "abolished death."[4] That is, he made it wholly inoperative, put it completely out of action.

Taking all the Scripture passages concerned, that clearly means three things. It means that spirit death is done away for all who come into touch with Jesus. It means further that during the kingdom time, actual death, meaning bodily

---

[1] John iii. 16; v. 21, 24; viii. 31; xi. 25.
[2] John vi. 39, 40, 44, 54.
[3] 1 Corinthians xv. 55-57.
[4] 1 Corinthians xv. 25, 26 (revised); 2 Timothy i. 10.

death, will cease on earth,[1] probably gradually until complete.

And the third meaning is this. There will be a final abolition or destroying of death for all, at the end of things on the earth.[2] That is, for all *except* Satan and anyone that incorrigibly insists on going his way.[3]

Death is put to death for all who will have it so. And it is so only because Christ suffered what we are spared.

[1] 1 Corinthians xv. 25-26.
[2] Revelations xxi. 4.
[3] Revelations xx. 14-15; xxi. 8.

VI

IS THERE ANOTHER CHANCE FOR SALVATION AFTER DEATH?

Four Common Answers

This is a question of chances. This talk will be a sober thoughtful study of chances. We say that every man should have a fair chance. That is ingrained in us.

The Britisher prides himself on his proverbial insistence on "fair play." And the American likes to think that that is one of his strongest traits, too. Underneath everything else, that is really the question here. Will every man have a "fair chance"? Will he get "fair play"?

That is to say, is God fair? Will he *be* fair with us when settling time comes? There've been some vigorous things said on the other side. Are these fair to God? God's good name has been slandered quite a bit. They say He will *not* give a man a fair chance. Are "they" right or wrong?

A chance is an opportunity. This is a question of *opportunity*. If you dig under that, it is really a question of a man's *use* of opportunity. Or rather, dig in just a bit deeper, it's a matter of keeping hold of our *ability* to use the opportunity.

For this touches directly one of the automatic laws of life. That is to say, what we don't use we lose. That is an inexorable law. What we can do, and don't do, by and by we lose the power to do. That "can" is lost. Failure to do steals away the power to do. If you refuse to use your eye, if you stay in the dark, by and by you can't use your eye. The seeing power is gone out of the eye. If you don't use any given set of muscles they go bad. You can't use them when you would.

The real question is this, will the man who has had full opportunity of making right choice here, and who has not used it, will he have another opportunity? Will the present opportunity be lengthened out beyond the grave? Or, digging deeper, if a man hasn't *used* his opportunity here, will his using power stick by him over there?

For, be it keenly marked, every man is master of his own destiny. He makes his own life. His present action controls his future. Every man is a prince in his own right. God said at the start, "have dominion" or mastery. Man is a master. He is masterful in his own action. He was made so. He is made so.

And so it can be said thoughtfully that *life is opportunity*. I mean to say this, and say it as strongly as I can, this: the biggest single thing in life is that it is an opportunity. If a man is alive, he has opportunity, opportunity to pick and choose, to decline and refuse, to go up or down. The earth is peculiarly the place of opportunity. Life is an open door to every man. The earth is an open door to every one on it.

Is this the reason why there is such a terrific

moral battle on here? Is this why the Evil One seems to be massing all his forces *now* and *here?* For it is clear enough that the earth is a battlefield, above all else, a tremendous moral battlefield. Every man's life is a battlefield. For the battle of earth is fought out and settled on the human battlefield of a man's life.

The black pencil mark is under that "another". Is there *another* chance? All life is a chance, as long as it may be, always long enough to use the opportunity it is. Is there another chance after this?

There are four common answers to this question. That fact of four shows how folks don't agree. Some say that one doesn't need another chance. No matter how we've used or not used our chance here, the thing goes only one way. We'll all pull through on the other side past any threatening dangers. And lately they have been adding, "We'll all pull through easily." Then there is an increasing number of those who say, quite positively, "Yes, there *is* another chance." Different groups gather here.

Strange to say, there are two separate "no" answers. And they come from two groups aggressively opposed to each other. Some say, "No, there's not another chance because if you haven't used your chance here, that's the end of you. You simply cease to exist. There's no other chance for you, because there's no "you" left to have another chance. This teaching is called "conditional immortality." Immortality or continued existence is conditioned on one's **re**lation to Christ, these teach.

The second "no" group puts the same general answer, but from a radically different angle. This is the old so-called orthodox group. Instead of another chance there is a ceaseless time of sleepless remorse over the unused chance. The tooth of pain never ceases cutting into your increasingly sensitive spirit, they say. The flame never burns out. It's a plain blunt "no," unadulterated, unmitigated, sometimes uttered in harsh forbidding tones.

The True Answer

What is *the true answer?* Is there an *authoritative* answer? Yes, there is. There is an authoritative Book. And *it* gives the one authoritative answer. It is the one source of *reliable information.* For we must have here not opinion, nor theory, nor wish. The thing is too serious. We must know authoritatively, *if* that's possible. Happily it is possible. The Book of God gives clear positive answer.

Let me at once give the Book's answer in a single sentence. Then we'll turn to the Book for its own specific statements. And the startling thing to note is this, that it doesn't agree directly with any one of these four answers. Though its answer comes to be practically the same in effect as one of them.

The Book's answer is this. *Yes and no: so far as the character of God's love is concerned there is another chance, that seemingly never runs out;* so far as a *man's decision is concerned there is no other chance.* And man's decision is the decisive thing there, as here. That seems undoubtedly to be the Book's own authoritative answer.

Now turn and look into the Book, for its detailed teachings. And the first question that comes up for its answer is this: *Is death the dividing line of opportunity?* Life is opportunity. When does that opportunity close? At death? Certainly death is a radical turning-point. When is the final decision rendered?

Listen to this word of Jesus: "If thy hand cause thee to stumble, cut it off; it is good for thee to enter into life (that is, the life beyond) maimed, rather than having two hands to go into Gehenna, into the unquenchable fire."

And then follows the emphasis of a repetition twice over, with variations of "foot" and "eye". And then this terrific underscoring, "where their worm dieth not, and the fire is not quenched."[1] Quite plainly our Lord teaches here that death is the decision time. It is the dividing line of opportunity. Life is opportunity; death is the close of opportunity.

Then there is another very decisive and explicit passage. It is the story of the rich man and the poor beggar in the Sixteenth of Luke.[2] That story is taken up rather fully in the third of these talks, "The Others." Clearly here death is the settlement time. At death each case is closed. And it is settled on its merits as it stands at that point. The award decided upon begins at the turning-point of death.

[1] Mark ix. 42-48.
[2] Luke xvi. 19-31.

Yet on the other hand, there's something else. This is not all the Scripture teaching. We want to be careful to get all, and then strike the balance. There is the striking passage in First Peter. There are two bits here that connect and run together. First comes this, speaking of Christ, "being put to death in the flesh, but made alive in the spirit; *in which* he also went and *preached to the spirits in prison,* that aforetime were disobedient, when the long suffering of God waited in the days of Noah," and so on.[1]

Note a few things about this passage. These spirits clearly were of men, human spirits, who had been disobedient to God's voice during their life on the earth, while Noah was building the ark. They had been swept away in the great cataclysm of the flood. And they are spoken of in the spirit world as being "in prison." This is the only place that that phrase is used for punishment in the next world.[2]

Now, it plainly says that Jesus went and preached to them. The word preached is that commonly used for preaching the Gospel. The plain inference of the connection is that while Jesus' body lay in Joseph's tomb, His spirit went on this gracious errand of mercy. He preached the message of the Father's love, and of His own sacrifice on Calvary, just made. The first preaching of the Calvary message was by the Calvary Man.

Then Peter picks up this thread again, a few lines further down. "For *unto this end was the*

[1] 1 Peter iii. 18-20; iv. 6.
[2] See however Jude, verse 6.

Gospel preached even to the dead, that they might *be judged* indeed according to men who are still in the flesh, but live according to God in the spirit."

Here is stated the *purpose* of the preaching. It was with a view to the coming time of judgment. It was to insure *perfect fairness* in the judging. There was to be full fair opportunity in order to a fair impartial judgment. The supposition at once is that these had not had that full opportunity essential to a fair just judgment in their cases. In the race-wide sweep of the terrible flood catastrophe that came, they had not had that fair chance.

And, at first flush, it would seem at once that these did have *another chance* for their salvation, after death. But a moment's thinking quickly indicates that it was not another. It was apparently their first opportunity. The whole swing of the connection makes that seem quite clear. It was the exquisite fairness of God giving them a chance which seemingly they had not had.

And, note further please, very keenly, *this is the only passage* of the sort in the whole Book of God. It stands out as the solitary lonely exception. This is immensely suggestive and significant. Thousands of passages, literally, urging right choice, and urging it *now;* one, just one, speaking by inference of a possible opportunity in the future life.

And the reference is incidental. For the main thing Peter is talking about is God's fairness in judgment. Teachers and educators will be keen to note the teaching principle here. Incessant repetition makes the essential thing stand out. The incidental drops practically out of view under the continued emphasis on the main point.

The Bible is an intensely practical book. It is a model in practical psychology, as well as in applied pedagogy. It is aiming continually at an immediate practical impression that shall influence one's decisions and life. It doesn't tell *all* the truth. It does tell all we need to know for right decision. And its whole insistent plea is this: Choose; choose the only right; choose it now, *now*.

God's Fixed Principle of Action

Take another look at the Book. There *is a principle underlying God's treatment of men* who set themselves against Him. It is a settled principle. He never varies from that principle by so much as the narrow width of a slender hair.

It is not a principle of punishment, *primarily*. Though the fact of punishment is tied up with it. It is not a using of God's superior power against these men. And it is not an *arbitrary* imposing of His will upon those unable to resist or get away. Indeed it is not an arbitrary principle in any way.

I use that word arbitrary in the good sense, of course. It may mean capricious or unreasoning. But in law it means such action or decision as is properly settled upon by the personal judgment of opinion of a judge or tribunal. It stands in contrast with decisions settled by certain established rules or equities. It should be noted that arbitrary action is recognized as quite proper. And God might act in what would be called an arbitrary way, with full justice and right.

Yet the principle that controls him is not arbitrary. It goes *deeper*. It has more of the heart element in it. I might say it has more of the good human element in it. I mean the sympathetic fellow-feeling element, that feels with a man in his difficulties and surroundings.

It is not on the level of law and right, merely. It is not merely what God *might properly do*. No, the controlling principle is up on the level of love, a strong controlling love. It is a matter of what He *prefers to do*. It is not the principle controlling a severe judge, perfectly proper in itself. It is rather the principle that controls *a wise father*.

Some one thinks here of that Twenty-fifth of Matthew. In the judgment scene depicted there, the King on the throne, who is the Son of Man Himself, acting as judge, says to some, "Depart; under a curse," and so on. That does indeed seem like a properly arbitrary judgment of the King.

Yet as one fits it in with all other passages dealing with the same matter, it is seen to be simply the judge's statement of how the scales swing. The judge holds the scale steady and true. The man's action tips them this way or that. The judge announces which way the scales tip. His action is recitative rather than arbitrary.

That fixed principle that controls God in His dealings with the man who sets himself against

God, as with all men, is this: *every man shall be utterly free to think and act as he chooses.* That was the dominating principle in Eden. It *is* the dominating principle as God breathes creative life and spirit being into every babe born. It will remain in absolute control in the future, wherever a man may choose to go. God has never taken that gift of free choice back. He never will.

To appreciate keenly how finely true this is one must brood over *the character of God.* He is not a judge, merely. He is that indeed, in the finest sense. But He is more than that word makes us think of. He is indeed, as the old phrase goes the moral Ruler of the universe. But with God the whole thing is on a higher, deeper, tenderer, humaner, level.

It will help get at the thing to recall some of the earlier ideas of the word "father". There are ideals inherent in the word which we westerners have lost, in some measure. The father was the *head* of the family. He ruled. There was no exception possible to his rulings. He was the *priest* of the family. He led its worship. He stood to the family for God, and stood to God for the family.

He was the *teacher,* instructing, disciplining, training and moulding. And with these, mingled inextricably was the tenderness of the father for his own child, companionship with the child, devotion to the child, an intense ambition and pleasure in the future of the child, and in an emergency any sacrifice needed for the sake of the child.

That old idea carried to its fullest degree, refined to the utmost, is the one word for God. He is peculiarly the Father. And be it keenly noted, He retains that relation *creatively* toward every man regardless of how that man treats God. He can't, of course, do all He would do except as the man voluntarily, gladly lets Him.

It will surely help here to make a contrast. Black put beside white looks blacker, or shows how black it really is. In contrast with the true meaning of father as seen in God, look at a *weak human father.*

David let his son, Amnon, go unrebuked and unpunished, though his wrong was as bad as bad could be. David let his favorite son Absalom also go free of rebuke or discipline or punishment. Yet Absalom was a murderer as Amnon was an adulterer. So lust and violence, two of the worst demons, were let loose in his kingdom.

Yet David was a wise ruler. But the father in him overcame the king in him. His emotion blurred his judgment. He *knew* full well *as king,* how evil the thing was, and how disastrous to his rule and kingdom. But the emotion in him dimmed his eye, and unsteadied his usually shrewd judgment. The result was that lust and blood ran riot. In the bad mix-up, he actually let the weakened fatherly traits in himself dethrone him as king. That's an illustration of weak fatherhood.

Two Flaming Proclamations

It will clear the ground, too, and help to sharper thinking, to remember the meaning of a phrase like *"the wrath of God."* It does *not* mean that God is angry in the common usage of that word. May I use a very homely phrase simply to make things clearer? It does *not* mean that He is "mad at you," in the common use of that term. Merely to put the thing that way makes it clear at once to thoughtful people that, of course, it does not. Yet may I remind you that the unthinking crowd unthinkingly has just that idea, especially when under the sway of some gifted religious demagogue.

Now, a little thinking into the character of God reveals the fact that the *wrath* of God is His purity blazing out against impurity. It is his fine sense of justice flaming out against rank injustice, His honesty burning as a fire against all dishonesty, deception, and trickery of every sort.

His wrath is never against *man,* except as the man gets so tangled up in the bad to which he's committed himself that the two are inseparable. "The wrath of God is revealed . . . against *all ungodliness* and *unrighteousness* of men."[1]

Now, look at the Scriptures on the principle that controls God in this matter. On *the very first leaf of the Book* man is entrusted with the power of free choice and action.[2] His continued good fellowship with God is conditioned on his own choice. Not to eat of the tree would keep him in touch with God. He is told not to eat. Yet it is a matter of choice. He *can* eat if he will. He has the ability.

Yet if he do, the break follows at once. "Dy-

[1] Romans i. 18.
[2] Genesis ii. 16, 17.

ing, thou shalt die"; a beginning, a process, a finished result. The worst result is plainly stated at once as a help and a warning. God Himself, man's Fellow in the garden, is the wooing by His mere presence, the pleading, that he do not eat of the tree. There would be separation. It would naturally be heart-breaking to God. There at the very start, is the statement of the fundamental principle of free choice.

On *the last page* of the Book is the same identical thing.[1] It is connected with that most winsome picture of the future life in the presence of God. But there's a bit of ugly black coloring in the picture. Then comes the bit emphasizing this unchangeable principle of God's great love for man, the principle of utter free choice.

Listen: "He that is set on being unrighteous, let him be wholly free to follow his choice, even here, and do unrighteousness." And the faithful warning word is graciously added, "and it will be with an ever increasing momentum."

"And he that is set in his choice to go on to the unrestrained depths of lustful passionate indulgence shall be left utterly free to follow his choice, and it will be found that the slant down gets steadily steeper and sharper."

Then the other side is put in the same two degrees. "He that is set in his choice to follow only the right and pure and good will be wholly free to follow the bent of his choice, with an ever increasing ease of movement upward."

"And he that chooses to climb the hill toward

[1] Revelation xxii. 11-15 paraphrased.

the highest peak of personal purity and holiness or wholeness, perfection of character, will have the fullest freedom in following his bent or choice. And he will find, too, the steepest heights more easily climbed as he goes up."

And when Jesus comes to straighten things out, He will give "to each man according as his choice has been." And his blessing is given those who have insisted on right choice in spite of difficulties and opposition. These now do the thing that goeth hand-in-hand with right choice. They go for cleansing to the blood of the Lamb.[1] And "without" are those whose choice leads and leaves them there.

Those two passages stand like two flaming proclamations at the beginning and end of this Book of God. He means that there shall be no ignorance nor mistake nor misunderstanding on this unwavering principle that controls Himself, this highest rarest gift of God to man, of free choice.

Now, all the way between, the Book is simply crammed with statements and illustrations of this same thing. Open almost anywhere, at random, and you will find pleadings to choose the right, warnings against persistence in wrong choice, and illustrations of those who do, and those who do not, make right choice.

Here then is the clear unmistakeable rare principle of strong love that controls God in His dealings with the man who is set against God's way of things. It is an unvarying principle. Love never faileth. It was so at the beginning.

[1] Revelation xxii 14 with vii. 14.

It has been kept up, unflagging, all along the way. It stays clear through to the unending end. Man's freedom of action is never interfered with by so much as half the breadth of a narrow hair.

The Process

Now it is fairly fascinating to find that *with this principle goes a process*. The two go together hand in glove. The principle of love is side by side with a rare process of love. I refer to the process by which a man goes to hell (the pen sticks with sheer pain at putting down the necessary words,) if he go.

He is not sent there. He is not put there. It is not a case of superior physical force taking possession of him, overcoming his resistance, and compelling him somewhere against his will. All human analogies, such as arrest by officers of the law, and enforced imprisonment in the penitentiaries, quite fail to tell the story here.

And further, it is not by any arbitrary action of God's, however fair and just it might be, by common consent. The process is simply this: *The man is left to himself*. What God does is this: He does nothing. He leaves the man to himself.

Now, the look into the Book. In the story of man's being put out of Eden it says of God, "so He drove out the man."[1] And the picture we have all had, pretty much is that of God in some forcible way driving Adam and Eve out, and

[1] Genesis iii. 24.

they reluctantly forced to yield to a power they could not withstand.

The same identical word is used by Cain on the other side of the page, "Behold, thou hast *driven* me out this day . . . and from thy face shall I be hid."[1] And one gets precisely the same picture as in the case of Adam and Eve.

But, mark thoughtfully, what it says a few lines further down in describing what actually took place: "And Cain *went out* from the presence of Jehovah."[2] This at once throws light on the expulsion from Eden, as well. That last sentence would naturally mean that there was no physical force used, but only moral.

The whole probability, practically to the point of certainty, is that Adam and Eve were greatly awed by God's presence and words. They were conscience-stricken, humiliated to the very dust. And they went out even as Cain. The sense of God's love and goodness to them, and his purity, and the bitter sense of their shame, their awful failure, the terrible break that they had caused between themselves and God, that sense and that only, drove them out. The whole fair presumption is that the sense of the character of God was so strong upon them that they walked out of their own accord, so far as any action on God's part was concerned, of the sort that we think of as physical.

This fits in perfectly with the very striking language Paul uses in that outstanding First of Romans. There is a terrific indictment of the

[1] Genesis iv. 14.
[2] Genesis iv. 16.

whole race in its sin of going its own way clean against God's way. And then Paul clearly states God's treatment of them.

Three times over its says *"God gave them up.*"[1] He did His best to restrain them. His love, His creative and sustaining and preserving care, His pleadings and wooings, were lavished on them. Then came the terrible words quoted, "He gave them up." He simply answered their tacit persistent prayer to be left alone. He left them alone. He left them to themselves. The process is quite clear.

A few years later, writing from Rome to the Ephesians, Paul traces *the steps in the process, on the human side,* by which a man goes away from God to his doom.[2] He says, "Walk no longer as the outsiders (Gentiles) also walk in the vanity of their mind, being darkened in their understanding, alienated from the life of God, because of the ignorance that is in them, because of the hardening of their heart; who being past feeling give themselves up to lasciviousness, to work all uncleanness with greediness."

The natural steps in the process are partially reversed here. He begins where the outsiders are at the time walking, or living the wrong sort of life. Then he traces the steps backward toward their starting-point, and adds the climax.

Let us put them in the order in which they naturally happen. First, there's the "hardening of the heart," or setting one's will against God. This results in their being "alienated," that is,

[1] Romans i. 24, 26, 28.
[2] Ephesians iv. 17-19.

cut off from God. Their action automatically cuts them off from God, but in their wilful ignorance they don't realize what they are doing.

Then quickly follows their being "darkened in their understanding." The whole mental processes are affected. The moral vision blurs. They call good evil, and evil good; darkness light and the reverse, and so on.[1] With this is joined naturally "the vanity of their minds." In failing to get things straight, they easily get full of their own ideas spun out of the fancy of their colored imaginations.

And this of course controls their "walk," that is, the practices of their daily life. And when this stage is reached, it quickly gets to the sad "past feeling" stage, morally. They give themselves up to unrestrained passion and lust. And the last, hardened stage is where lust is traded in for sordid gain. The whole movement, it will be thoughtfully noticed is automatic. It is the natural logical staircase downward. And that is describing things *in this life*. It is like that here. What will it be *there?* Here, now, grace still influences, even though resisted. There, then, it apparently is quite kept out, shut out.

Jesus' treatment of Judas that betrayal night sheds a flood of light here.[2] There was the utmost effort to keep Judas *in*. The plainspoken warning Judas instantly recognized as meant for himself. Then there's the bit of tender personal love-touch in handing Judas the tid-

[1] See Isaiah v. 20.
[2] John xiii. 21-30.

bit, the first morsel from the dish containing the simple evening meal.

But Judas hardens his heart against warnings and tender pleadings alike. That hardening, which was a shutting out of God, was a letting in of some one else. Then Judas, bent on carrying his purpose, rises and goes out. And it was black night out where he had gone.

A Dramatic Illustration

It will be noticed that these passages all have to do with the present life. And we are talking about the future life. But these reveal *God's habit* in dealing with men. And at heart, this is a question about God: Will God be fair? In the common talk of the crowd, "will God play fair?"

These passages show how God does *now*. They do more. They show the *principle* that controls Him in his dealings. We see His unvarying insistence of man being free to choose. And they show the *process* that works out under that principle. Unless there are some specific statements in the Book regarding a change of principle and process we would naturally look for this treatment to continue beyond the grave. And, be it carefully noted, there are no such specific statements.

But, now, we turn to another sort of passage. It is the story of Pharaoh in Egypt. And it should be keenly noted that here God is *dealing in judgment*. That is, He is acting to settle-up long-standing wrongs, and to straighten them out.

The Hebrews had been wronged in the most grievous way for several generations. The Pharaohs had oppressed them with increasing heartless severity. There had been a long period of long-suffering by God toward the Pharaohs. Now a settlement time has come. That is what judgment, in principle, is.

There are now specific warnings and requests and pleadings with Pharaoh before action is taken finally. Then comes a carefully graduated series of transactions that constitute a visitation of judgments upon Egypt. They grow steadily from less to greater, from bad to worse. And there's always an interval between times to give Pharaoh opportunity to make the changes needed.

There is a significant word here. It seems to be used about nineteen times in a brief space. It's the word "harden," in varying forms. God says, "I will harden his (Pharaoh's) heart."[1] Nine times it says, with some variations, that He hardened Pharaoh's heart.[2] And five times it says that Pharaoh hardened his heart, or was stubborn.[3]

That hardening was, and is, an unnatural thing, though so common. Man was created to live in touch with God. Out of that touch he is out of his native environment. And he doesn't act as he naturally would. Pharaoh had persistently shut God's pleadings with his inner

---

[1] Exodus iv. 21; vii. 3; xiv. 4, 17.
[2] Exodus vii. 13, 14, 22; ix. 12, 35; x. 20, 27; xi. 10; xiv. 8.
[3] Exodus viii. 15, 19, 32; ix. 7, 34.

heart, and God's presence, *out*. He cut himself off from that influence which would have made him act in a true human natural way. The result is expressed in this significant way. His heart was hardened or heavy. It was stubbornly set. And it says distinctly that he sinned in this very thing of hardening himself against God.[1]

He had been doing this for long. Now the decision time has come. God purposes to let the Egyptians and the Hebrews and the world know directly of His rejected scorned power. He simply now withdraws some of the creative touch He has been keeping on Pharaoh. Some of his gracious restraint is withdrawn. That is all. He doesn't do anything except to stop, partly, what He has been doing.

The visitation of judgment runs through plagues or pests, disease, storms, the death of every Egyptian first-born son, and the drowning of the Egyptian army. In each case it is quite possible that the action came simply through the withdrawal of divine restraint. And everything of the sort in the Book favors the supposition that that was the way it did come.

In the case of the first-born dead there was nothing that the Egyptians could see that happened to kill their heirs. They simply knew that the babe or boy or young man was found lying dead in his bed.

In the case of the army drowning the wind blew back the waters. It was a special act of

[1] Exodus ix. 34.

God's power on behalf of His people. He held the waters back. When they were safe, that power was withdrawn. The law of gravity pulled the waters back again. The Egyptians in their headstrong rage put themselves in danger. The danger materialized. The waters swamped them. The *process* was wholly a natural one.

Now, this is more than history. It is teaching, picture teaching. It's a triple picture. It's a picture of God's patience, the most marked trait of His character in the whole story. It's a picture of the obstinate headstrong stubborn will of a man, out of his native element, God's gracious presence. It's a picture of the principle and process in judgment.

There are certain *apparent* partial exceptions to this law of action. It *seems* like arbitrary action on God's part in the flood that destroys the whole race, except eight persons; and in the terrific lightning-storm that wiped out Sodom and the other cities of the Plain.

But it is not at all clear that there was arbitrary action. It is impossible to know. And if so, it extended simply to the *time* element involved. Sin left to itself burns itself out. There seems here simply a *shortening* of the time involved in the natural process.

And maybe not even that, for there may have been a patiently extended restraint that prevented disaster from coming earlier. Then the restraint withdrawn, nature's process worked out naturally, and maybe faster through the acceleration of long restraint withdrawn.

Let it be thoughtfully marked that God has hung up these and other danger signals in full view. The train I was on the other day ran by a large powder factory. And everywhere about the place I could read, even as we hurried by, the warnings in large letters against "matches" and the like. We ran by some out-buildings of the railroad company, with stringent warnings in plain view against inflammables because of the contents of these buildings.

God's danger signals are in big bold letters, hung up where all the race can read. The Dead Sea is a warning signal, known to all. It's the deepest ugliest scar on the earth's surface. No life can exist there, neither animal nor vegetable. It points out the *fact* of *judgment* on *wrong*.

But there's something closer by. Nature's common laws are inexorable, mercilessly inexorable, aye, because merciless therefore merciful, mercifully inexorable. The fire mercilessly burns your hand if you stick it in. Instantly you snatch it out. The pain mercifully leads you to keep your whole arm from the flame.

In contrast, man's laws are notoriously loose. And so the contagion of evil spreads. One murderer acquitted is followed by other murders. It never fails. Failure to uphold the dignity of law leads to a lowered moral tone in the community, inevitably. A king or a president, loose in his personal morality, always leads the crowd down the same incline. Nature's laws are merciful because they are so merciless. The warning signals are at hand everywhere,

This then traces the process of God's dealing with the man who sets himself against God. It is a process of patient strong love on God's part, and of reluctant witholding of what is being rejected. It is a process of terrible de-gradation on man's part, gradation downwards.

A Study in Chances

And now we swing back to our starting point on this talk. It is really quite accurate to say that this is a study of chances. That is to say, technically, theoretically, the thing is not settled at death. It is *never* settled. The way is always open for another chance. That statement is logically technically, accurate. Underscore *technically*. Technically means so far as the *points* of logic are concerned.

But what about *actually?* The man on the street is impatient of theory. He is concerned only with the *practical*. And so now we will discuss the thing wholly from the practical, the common sense point of view. *What are a man's chances who passes out of this life without taking advantage of his opportunity Godward?*

And the answer to this is very plain and positive. You know that there is now a science of chances. At least it is reckoned a science for all practical, that is to say, for money-making purposes. The great life insurance and assurance companies have experts on chances. And the huge volume of business they transact, involving billions of dollars, is based wholly on the findings of these experts.

These men are called actuaries. An actuary

is one skilled in the doctrine and practice of chances as applied to human life. They calculate your chance of life in the most critical impersonal dispassionate way. They have the whole subject of chances down to a science. That is, down to the point of definite knowledge of certain facts and tendencies. They have worked out a law of chances. It is with them purely a matter of money.

Now let me say soberly that there is here a study in the science of chances. And when you sift the thing down to the last word, the final word is not spoken by God. It is spoken by the man concerned. It is wholly a matter of his choice.

It can be said, very thoughtfully, that so far as God is concerned, judging simply from His character as revealed in this Book, that there is never a time when a man turning to God in true penitence would not find God's door wide open.

But, *but,* the probability or chance of a man changing his choice is so extremely remote that it can be said in the most positive terms that there is not another chance beyond the grave. The matter rests with the man. And he won't give himself the chance.

The man who doesn't do to-day, what he knows in his heart he should do, is—are you listening very quietly?—is, let me say it very quietly, but as plainly as English can put it, he is playing the part of a—it's a hard word to say, but it's literally a true word, so it must be said, even though saying it gives sharpest pain, *he is playing the part of a fool.*

He *is* a fool, and not even a bright fool. He is playing a losing game. That means a lost game. He is still playing but the game is settled by the law of chance, and settled lost. That is not simply using strong language. It is really an understatement. The word fool is less than what the man is.

Why do I say that? Listen very thoughtfully, and I will tell you why. It is easier to make the right choice to-day than it will be to-morrow. It will be actually harder to-morrow. No, that isn't simply good Methodist exhorting. That's true, as a mere bit of pure psychology. It's a scientific statement according to the fixed law of chances.

Let me explain why. You see the whole thing depends on the thing in the man that does the choosing. If he knows to-day, by the inner feel, that he should accept Jesus as his Saviour, with all that that means, and he doesn't do it, he is making a decision. He is choosing. He is choosing not to choose.

That act of choosing affects his choosing power. It becomes at once a bit more set in its way, the way he has set it. It's like a bit of cement, it begins to harden. You say, "O, yes, but it's very slight." Yes, but however slight, it is so. He has a tougher task to-morrow. That inner pull is offset.

And every to-morrow the thing gets more set. It grows unlikelier every day that he will do that bit of choosing, simply because, just now, the choosing power is harder set the other way. **If you** do a thing once you *can* do it *again*. And you are likely to. You will do it faster and more easily, and better or more decidedly or more skilfully.

Now let that go on for years, and then keep going on beyond the grave. And it comes to the point where he can't change. Theoretically he can. So far as God is concerned the way is open to him. Actually he can't. The choosing power is hardened beyond change. When he could, he wouldn't. Now he can't. And note sharply, he doesn't want to.

It isn't to say that now when he would he can't; not that. He still can, so far as God is concerned, but he does not want to. He wants to get away from the suffering, working out of his insistent choice. But he doesn't want to get into normal touch with God, through the crucified Christ.

This is the "great gulf fixed," the impassable gulf. The rich man in Luke Sixteenth evinced no desire to change his choice. There was no change in his attitude toward God nor toward his own selfish life on the earth. The only thing distressing him was the pain he was suffering. He wanted to get rid of that. That was all.

For notice how that choosing power in a man is limbered up so it can reverse itself. It is *not* by some act of judgment, *nor* by pain, *nor* suffering of any sort. All evidence makes it quite clear that these things of themselves do not soften; they harden. It is only God's gracious softening mellowing touch that can unlimber that hardened stiffened rusted will. And that's shut out. The man has shut out the one thing that would normalize his choosing faculty and help him change his choice.

Love Never Faileth

And so this authoritative Book makes very positive statements about the terrible final result for the man who insists on leaving God out, or openly antagonizes His rule. The Book has a distinctive way of putting things. It is a popular book, in the best sense of that word. It is, of course, an Oriental book. And that is the same thing as saying that it is a book for the common crowd of men everywhere.

The Oriental mode of thought and expression is really photographic. That is, it catches a picture at one point only. It states final fixed results, but doesn't go to giving the process by which that result is reached.

The characteristic western way is different. I mean the cultured scholarly way. I could say the book way as distinct from the common way of the crowd. It goes to processes. It analyzes and dissects the process by which the result is reached. It is more like the moving picture photographs, giving the story in successive steps.

There's a distinct touch of divine wisdom and insight in the use of this Oriental mode in the make-up of the Bible. For this is the common mode of thought and expression, not only of the Oriental world to this day, *but,* broader, the common method of the crowds everywhere, in western civilized lands as well as in the uncivilized and half-civilized lands.

And so the Book in its rare wisdom puts the thing in the way that is instantly understood by the common people everywhere around the world, and by all others, too. It states the final result. And it is found to be the result which we have found here at the end of our study of the process. It is the result reached by the specialist in the law of probability. It makes a profound impression upon a man studying the process to find the rare accuracy and the profound human wisdom of the statements of this old Book.

Listen to its simple, tremendously positive, language. "He that believeth not (or disbelieveth) shall be damned (or condemned)."[1] "He that believeth (or obeyeth) not the son *shall not see life,* but the *wrath of God abideth on him.*"[2] "These shall go away into *everlasting* (or eternal) *punishment.*"[3] These are authoritative statements of this Book of God. And they are fully concurred in by the human law of probabilities.

And so very thoughtfully you repeat the answer to the question. Is there another chance after death? *Yes, and no. So far as the character of God's love is concerned there is another chance, a chance that seemingly never runs out. So far as man's decision is concerned there is not another chance.* And man's decision is the decisive thing. God leaves the matter with a man's free choice. He insists that a man shall stay up

[1] Mark xvi. 16.
[2] John iii. 36.
[3] Matthew xxv. 46.

on the original level of free choice and action.

And so the last word, on the last page in the old Book, is a pleading word. It is spoken by the Man who died. He cried out earnestly, "He that *will,* *let* him *take* the water of life freely."[1]

The legend is told of a French mother who loved her son with a tense unselfish devotion. But he was caught by the wildfire of lust, and the flames burned deep. He came under the fascination of a rarely beautiful but utterly heartless bad woman. The mother held on to her son with love's tenacity and pleadings. The evil woman was enraged that she was not able to wipe out completely the mother's influence. In an evil hour, when her spell was strong, she got the young man's promise to bring to her the heart of his mother.

The legend pictures him keeping the promise. He was hurrying to his appointment with the evil charmer, with the bundle under his arm that contained his mother's heart. He stumbled and fell. And at once the voice he knew so well spoke with tender solicitude out of the bleeding heart, *"Oh, my son, are you hurt?"* There was no reproach; only love; love's concern; undying self-effacing love.

A legend; yes, but it is true to life. It pictures the true mother. He could kill her, but he couldn't kill her love, nor still her voice. The mother love is the greatest human love known. The true mother-heart comes the nearest to God's heart.

[1] Revelation xxii. 17 l. c.

God suffers when any creative child of his suffers. He suffers more over any one going to hell than the man who goes suffers. The man's capacity for finer suffering grows less. The finer feelings grow gross. God's suffering increases. But he won't rob man of his highest power, free choice, even to lessen his own suffering.

God's love never faileth. It can't. It won't.

BIBLE STUDY

P. WHITWELL WILSON *Author of "The Christ We Forget"*

The Church We Forget

A Study of the Life and Words of the Early Christians. 8vo, cloth, net

The author of "The Christ We Forget" here furnishes a companion-picture of the earliest Christian Church—of the men and women, of like feelings with ourselves, who followed Christ and fought His battles in the Roman world of their day. "Here again," says Mr. Wilson, "my paint-box is the Bible, and nothing else—and my canvas is a page which he who runs may read."

C. ALPHONSO SMITH, Ph.D., LL.D.

Head of the Department of English in the U. S. Naval Academy, Annapolis, Md.

Key-note Studies in Key-note Books of the Bible 12mo, cloth, net

The sacred books dealt with are Genesis, Esther, Job, Hosea, John's Gospel, Romans, Philippians, Revelation. "No series of lectures yet given on this famous foundation have been more interesting and stimulating than these illuminating studies of scriptural books by a layman and library expert."—*Christian Observer.*

GEORGE D. WATSON, D.D.

God's First Words

Studies in Genesis, Historic, Prophetic and Experimental. 12mo, cloth, net

Dr. Watson shows how God's purposes and infinite wisdom, His plan and purpose for the race, His unfailing love and faithfulness are first unfolded in the Book of Genesis, to remain unchanged through the whole canon of Scripture. Dr. Watson's new work will furnish unusual enlightment to every gleaner in religious fields, who will find "God's First Words" to possess great value and profit.

EVERETT PEPPERRELL WHEELER, A.M.

Author of "Sixty Years of American Life," etc.

A Lawyer's Study of the Bible

Its Answer to the Questions of To-day. 12mo, cloth, net

Mr. Wheeler's main proposition is that the Bible, when wisely studied, rightly understood and its counsel closely followed, is found to be of inestimable value as a guide to daily life and conduct. To this end Mr. Wheeler examines its teachings as they relate to sociology, labor and capital, socialism, war, fatalism, prayer, immortality. A lucid, helpful book.

THE NEW WORLD ORDER

JOSEPH FORT NEWTON, D.D.

Pastor of The Church of the Divine Paternity, New York

The Religious Basis of a Better World Order

By the Author of "An Ambassador," etc. 12mo.

"These sermons speak especially to cultivated minds, yet through their simplicity and naturalness and humanness, they make the universal appeal. Here is their real power. They do not speak the language of the church, but the language of humanity. They are real sermons of a warm, spiritual, enthusiastic manhood."—*American Journal of Theology.*

HENRY CHURCHILL KING   *President of Oberlin College*

A New Mind for the New Age

Cole Lectures for 1920. 12mo.

President King's new book is the work of one whose opinions are of great weight in these times of uncertainty and doubt. Contents: I. The New Age: Its Evidence. II. The New Age: Its Perils. III. The New Age: Its Values. IV. The New Mind: The Political Challenge. V. The New Mind: The Educational Challenge. VI. The New Mind: The Religious Challenge.

ROBERT WELLS VEACH, M.A., D.D.

Associate Director Department of Social Service New Era Movement

The Meaning of the War for Religious Education

12mo.

"A Book for our Day. It begins and ends right and deals with the elements of reconstruction wisely and in the right order. The book is strong, the argument appealing, the conclusion inevitable and the spirit optimistic. It is just the kind of a book the Church needs to read and act upon in these strategic days of social unrest and world reconstruction."—*Marion Lawrance.*

JAMES E. FREEMAN, D.D.

Rector of St. Mark's Church, Minneapolis, Minn.

Everyday Religion

Little "Minneapolis Tribune" Sermons. 12mo, cloth.

Here is a "live" volume of addresses particularly. The themes have direct bearing on the problems of every day existence in these critical, heart-searching days. The work cannot fail to furnish stimulus and enheartenment for all who recognize the deeper and larger problems of life.